Help for Adolescent Males with Sexual Behavior Problems

Treatments That Work
TM

Help for Adolescent Males with Sexual Behavior Problems

A COGNITIVE-BEHAVIORAL TREATMENT PROGRAM

Workbook

John A. Hunter

OXFORD
UNIVERSITY PRESS

2011

OXFORD
UNIVERSITY PRESS

Oxford University Press, Inc., publishes works that further
Oxford University's objective of excellence
in research, scholarship, and education.

Oxford New York
Auckland Cape Town Dar es Salaam Hong Kong Karachi
Kuala Lumpur Madrid Melbourne Mexico City Nairobi
New Delhi Shanghai Taipei Toronto

With offices in
Argentina Austria Brazil Chile Czech Republic France Greece
Guatemala Hungary Italy Japan Poland Portugal Singapore
South Korea Switzerland Thailand Turkey Ukraine Vietnam

Published by Oxford University Press, Inc.
198 Madison Avenue, New York, New York 10016

www.oup.com

ISBN-13 978-0-19-532950-6 Paper

About Treatments *ThatWork*™

One of the most difficult problems confronting patients with various disorders and diseases is finding the best help available. Everyone is aware of friends or family who have sought treatment from a seemingly reputable practitioner, only to find out later from another doctor that the original diagnosis was wrong or the treatments recommended were inappropriate or perhaps even harmful. Most patients, or family members, address this problem by reading everything they can about their symptoms, seeking out information on the Internet, or aggressively "asking around" to tap knowledge from friends and acquaintances. Governments and health care policymakers are also aware that people in need don't always get the best treatments—something they refer to as "variability in healthcare practices."

Now healthcare systems around the world are attempting to correct this variability by introducing "evidence-based practice." This simply means that it is in everyone's interest that patients get the most up-to-date and effective care for a particular problem. Healthcare policymakers have also recognized that it is very useful to give consumers of healthcare as much information as possible, so that they can make intelligent decisions in a collaborative effort to improve health and mental health. This series, Treatments *That Work*™ is designed to accomplish just that. Only the latest and most effective interventions for particular problems are described in user-friendly language. To be included in this series, each treatment program must pass the highest standards of evidence available, as determined by a scientific advisory board. Thus, when individuals suffering from these problems or their family members seek out an expert clinician who is familiar with these interventions and decides that they are appropriate, they will have confidence that they are receiving the best care available. Of course, only your health care professional can decide on the right mix of treatments for you.

This workbook is designed for your use as you work in a group with other adolescent males who have committed sexual offenses. Treatment is not punishment, but a way for you to learn new skills and make positive changes in how you make decisions and live your life.

This program is organized into three phases. In Phase I, you will learn how to improve your social skills and how to control your sexual impulses. In Phase II you will learn effective anger management skills and about healthy sexuality. In Phase III you will learn about empathy and how to avoid relapse after treatment has ended.

Successful completion of treatment will help ensure that you do not make the same mistakes again, and go on to live a healthy and productive life.

David H. Barlow, Editor-in-Chief,
Treatments *ThatWork*™
Boston, MA

Contents

Chapter 1 *Getting Started*

Introduction to the Program

You are about to begin a treatment program designed specifically for adolescent males with sexual behavior problems. You may be nervous or scared about starting this program, and that is normal. Please remember, however, that treatment is not punishment. Treatment is about learning new skills and making positive changes in how you make decisions and live your life. Successful completion of treatment will help ensure that you do not make the same mistakes again and go on to live a healthy and productive life.

Over the course of several months, you will meet with a group of your peers who all share similar experiences. You will work together to understand your thoughts and behaviors, and to practice new ways of relating to others and handling problems. One of the most important things that you will learn is that you are not alone in having to address sexual behavior problems. Lots of boys your age have faced and overcome these issues.

Treatment is organized into three phases. In Phase I, you will learn how to improve your social skills and how to control your sexual impulses. You will also be introduced to the concept of *healthy masculinity,* which is a concept you will learn about through all of the phases of this program. In Phase II, you will learn effective anger management skills and about healthy sexuality. In Phase III, you will learn about empathy and how to avoid relapse after treatment has ended.

Although it may not be your choice to participate in this program, it is important that you understand its benefits. The majority of youths who successfully complete treatment do not sexually reoffend, and they go on to lead normal and productive lives. You, too, can be successful—if you stay motivated and work hard.

Use of the Workbook

This workbook contains all the information and materials you will need throughout treatment. It includes summaries of topics you will discuss in sessions with your therapist, as well as homework assignments and the forms you need to complete them. Although you are required to complete homework assignments, you will not be graded on them. It is very important to do your best to complete the assignments, however. Practicing the skills you learn on a regular basis is key to your success.

Before your first session, review this chapter and write down any questions you have about the program in the space provided so you can discuss them with your therapist. Be sure to bring your workbook to every session.

Phase I

Chapter 2 *Social Skills*

Introduction

Many males your age who engage in sexually abusive behavior have problems forming and maintaining healthy relationships with others. The focus of the first part of treatment is to help you improve your social and communication skills. We want to help you develop self-confidence and the ability to make friends and resolve conflicts. You will also learn how to handle rejection and disappointment so that you do not become angry or aggressive.

INTRODUCTION OF SOCIAL SKILLS

Goals

- To learn about social skills
- To understand the importance of social skills
- To complete the social skills pre-test

What Are Social Skills?

Social skills are the set of skills people use to interact and communicate with one another. Having good social skills means you are able to successfully communicate with others and effectively express your feelings and needs. It also means that you are able to detect and understand what other people want and need. Social skills serve as the foundation for healthy human interactions and help us learn to work with and relate to others.

Why Are Social Skills Important?

Social skills are important because they can help you meet interesting people, form healthy relationships, and accomplish your goals in life. Good social skills can also help you avoid conflicts and settle arguments.

Think about why good social skills are important in each of the following areas. Write down your thoughts in the space provided

Parent-child relationships

____

____

____

Making friends

____

____

____

Getting and keeping a job

____

____

____

Succeeding in school

____

____

____

Social Skills and Sexual Offending

Think about how poor social skills may have contributed to your offense. If you do not have good social skills, you may feel angry, frustrated, or resentful, and this can lead to poor decisions and inappropriate actions. Because of poor social skills, you may have misinterpreted your victim's behavior or misread his or her feelings. Your therapist will discuss the role of social skills in sexual offending with you in more detail. It is important to note however, that mastery of basic social skills can lower your risk of reoffending and improve the overall quality of your life.

Social Skills Pre-Test

At the beginning of each module, your therapist will ask you to take a "pre-test." The tests are designed to evaluate your progress and to inform your therapist whether you are ready to move to the next module of the program.

The first test you will take is called the Social Skills Pre-Test. Your therapist will hand out copies of the test to you and the other members of the group. He or she will collect them and review the results with you at your next meeting. These tests will help you and your therapist set your treatment goals.

Homework

✎ Complete the Social Skills Pre-Test

PRE-TEST RESULTS AND TREATMENT GOALS

Goal

- To go over your pre-test results and set goals for treatment

My Treatment Goals

Together with your therapist, use the space provided to develop your treatment goals and list them in order of importance.

My Treatment Goals—Social Skills Module

1. ______________________________
2. ______________________________
3. ______________________________
4. ______________________________
5. ______________________________

Homework

✎ Review your goals with your therapist and bring them to your next meeting.

LISTENING SKILLS

Goals

- To understand the importance of listening skills
- To learn the critical components of listening
- To practice your listening skills

Why are Listening Skills Important?

Being a good listener is an important social skill. Listening well helps you to learn from others and to understand other people's feelings and needs. If you are a poor listener, you may have trouble learning new skills and understanding what someone else expects of you (e.g., your parent, your teacher, or your boss). If you don't listen well, other people may think that you aren't interested in their opinions or what they have to say. Poor listening can result in poor performance at school or at work and alienation from others.

Think about times when you didn't listen properly to others and when others failed to listen to you. What happened in both circumstances? How did you feel? How do you think the other person felt?

Critical Components of Listening

There are several ways you can tell when someone is really listening to you. Are they making eye contact? Are they asking you questions about what you are saying? These are all behaviors that show a person is actively listening and using good listening skills. The following is a list of things you should be doing when practicing good listening.

- Making eye contact with the person who is speaking
- Maintaining appropriate body posture (i.e., don't slouch or turn away from the person who is speaking)
- Thinking about what the other person is saying
- Showing that you are listening by nodding your head and commenting on what the person is saying (e.g., "I understand.")
- Asking clarifying questions, as needed ("I'm not sure I understand; tell me more about so-and-so.")
- Being patient and choosing the right time to talk
- When speaking, clearly expressing feelings and thoughts about the subject

Practicing Good Listening Skills

In this meeting with your therapist, you and other members of the group will participate in role-plays in which you will have the chance to practice good listening skills. Some ideas for role-plays are:

- having a conversation with a friend who is describing a movie or book that he really liked
- a teacher is giving a homework assignment
- a parent is assigning household chores

Your therapist will work with you to choose an appropriate role-play and will give you feedback on your "performance." You will also rate your performance and have your role-play partner rate your performance, using the Role-Play Recording Form provided. Be sure to practice the good listening behaviors you learned in the previous section.

Homework

✎ Practice good listening skills as often as possible.

Role-Play Recording Form

Date: ___________

Rehearsed skill: ______________________________

Role-play partner: ____________________________ (e.g., staff member, peer, parent, etc.)

Self-rating of comfort/competency

Circle the number that best represents how well you feel you did in performing the role-play.

1. (felt very uncomfortable and awkward)
2. (felt mildly uncomfortable and awkward)
3. (felt fairly comfortable; adequate performance)
4. (felt generally comfortable; good performance)
5. (felt very comfortable; excellent performance)

Partner rating of comfort/competency

Circle the number that best represents how well you feel your partner did in performing the role-play.

1. (he seemed very uncomfortable and unsure of himself)
2. (he appeared mildly uncomfortable and unsure of himself)
3. (he appeared fairly comfortable; adequate performance)
4. (he appeared generally comfortable; good performance)
5. (he appeared very comfortable; excellent performance)

Goals

- To understand the importance of conversation skills
- To learn the critical components of starting a conversation
- To practice your conversation skills

Why Are Conversation Skills Important?

Being able to easily start a conversation with a peer is an important social skill. This skill will help you get to know others and make new friends. If you are unable to start a conversation, you may end up feeling left out or uncomfortable in social situations. You also may become afraid of meeting new people.

Critical Components of Starting a Conversation

The following is a list of the steps you should take when attempting to start a conversation. If you follow these steps, you are sure to be successful.

1. Choose the right time and place.
2. Make eye contact with the person you are speaking to.
3. Smile and greet the other person in a friendly way (e.g., Say "hi" and shake hands).
4. Make casual conversation (talk about sports, school, weather, music, etc.).
5. Check to see if the other person is listening (e.g., making eye contact, commenting, or nodding)
6. Bring up your question or the topic you would like to talk about (e.g., "I was wondering if you would like to play basketball after school?").

Practicing Conversation Skills

As you did in the previous meeting, you and other members of the group will participate in role-plays in which you will have the chance to practice conversation skills. Some ideas for role-plays are introducing yourself to someone at a party and asking a classmate to come over to your house after school.

Your therapist will work with you to choose an appropriate role-play and will give you feedback on your "performance." Remember to rate your performance, and have your partner do the same, using the Role-Play Recording Form provided. Be sure to practice the steps you learned in the previous section.

Homework

 Try to start a conversation with one of your peers whom you don't know very well. Use the skills you learned in this section.

Role-Play Recording Form

Date: __________

Rehearsed skill: ______________________________

Role-play partner: ____________________________ (e.g., staff member, peer, parent, etc.)

Self-rating of comfort/competency

Circle the number that best represents how well you feel you did in performing the role-play.

1. (felt very uncomfortable and awkward)
2. (felt mildly uncomfortable and awkward)
3. (felt fairly comfortable; adequate performance)
4. (felt generally comfortable; good performance)
5. (felt very comfortable; excellent performance)

Partner rating of comfort/competency

Circle the number that best represents how well you feel your partner did in performing the role-play.

1. (he seemed very uncomfortable and unsure of himself)
2. (he appeared mildly uncomfortable and unsure of himself)
3. (he appeared fairly comfortable; adequate performance)
4. (he appeared generally comfortable; good performance)
5. (he appeared very comfortable; excellent performance)

ASKING QUESTIONS

Goals

- To understand the importance of asking questions
- To learn the critical components of asking questions
- To practice asking questions

Why Is Asking Questions Important?

Being able to ask questions is an important social skill. It is rare in new learning situations, or social interactions, that a person can completely understand the material or the topics being discussed without asking questions. If you don't ask questions, you are limiting your ability to learn and be successful. What would happen if you were afraid to ask questions at school or at work? You might not complete your assignments or duties correctly, which could lead your teacher or boss to think that you are distracted or that you are not trying your best.

Critical Components of Asking Questions

Following is a list of the critical components of asking questions.

1. Decide what you'd like to learn more about. It may be something you don't understand or is confusing (e.g., a math problem or directions to a place you've never been before.) It could also be asking for a privilege, such as permission to use your parents' car or go to a party.
2. Decide who would be the best source of information. In deciding this, think about who has the best information on the subject and/or who has the authority to answer your question. Remember, you may want to ask more than one person to make sure that you have reliable information (e.g., directions to the airport).

3. Think about possible ways to ask your question and choose the one that feels most comfortable.
4. Decide the best time and place to ask the question (e.g., wait for a pause in the conversation, wait for privacy).
5. Ask your question in a friendly and positive manner. Make good eye contact while speaking and be sure to smile.
6. If the person doesn't have the answer to your question, ask them to identify someone who might have the answer.
7. Thank the person for answering (or trying to answer) your question.

Practicing Asking Questions

As you have been doing, you and other members of the group will participate in role-plays in which you will have the chance to practice asking questions. Some ideas for role-plays are asking for directions and asking a teacher to explain a homework assignment.

Remember to complete the Role-Play Recording Form.

Homework

✎ Look for opportunities to ask questions in everyday life. Use the skills you learned in this section.

Role-Play Recording Form

Date: ___________

Rehearsed skill: ______________________________

Role-play partner: ____________________________ (e.g., staff member, peer, parent, etc.)

Self-rating of Comfort/Competency

Circle the number that best represents how well you feel you did in performing the role-play.

1. (felt very uncomfortable and awkward)
2. (felt mildly uncomfortable and awkward)
3. (felt fairly comfortable; adequate performance)
4. (felt generally comfortable; good performance)
5. (felt very comfortable; excellent performance)

Partner Rating of Comfort/Competency

Circle the number that best represents how well you feel your partner did in performing the role-play.

1. (he seemed very uncomfortable and unsure of himself)
2. (he appeared mildly uncomfortable and unsure of himself)
3. (he appeared fairly comfortable; adequate performance)
4. (he appeared generally comfortable; good performance)
5. (he appeared very comfortable; excellent performance)

Goals

- To understand the importance of being able to introduce yourself and others
- To learn the critical components of introductions
- To practice introducing yourself and others

Why Are Introduction Skills Important?

Being able to introduce yourself is a necessary social skill. It is also important to know how to introduce others. These skills can help you feel more comfortable in new situations (e.g., going to a new school, starting a new job) and can help you meet new people and make new friends. They also show others that you are confident.

Critical Components of Introducing Yourself

Following is a list of the critical components of introducing yourself.

1. Pick the best time and place to introduce yourself (e.g., the person does not appear busy or already involved in some activity).
2. Smile and seem friendly as you approach the person.
3. Say "hi" to the person and tell them your name (shake hands if appropriate).
4. Ask the person his or her name, if you don't know it.
5. Make a statement or ask the other person something to help start the conversation (e.g., tell something about yourself; comment on something you have in common; ask a question).
6. Show that you are interested in what the person is saying by making good eye contact and nodding your head.

7. When ending the conversation, let the person know that you are pleased to have made his or her acquaintance.
8. If you liked the person, suggest when you might see him or her again.

Practicing Introducing Yourself

Like you have been doing, you and other members of the group will participate in role-plays in which you will have the chance to introduce yourselves. Some ideas for role-plays are meeting a new resident participant in the program, introducing yourself to new classmates, and introducing yourself to new teammates.

Remember to complete the Role-Play Recording Form.

Role-Play Recording Form

Date: ___________

Rehearsed skill: ______________________________

Role-play partner: ____________________________ (e.g., staff member, peer, parent, etc.)

Self-rating of Comfort/Competency

Circle the number that best represents how well you feel you did in performing the role-play.

1. (felt very uncomfortable and awkward)
2. (felt mildly uncomfortable and awkward)
3. (felt fairly comfortable; adequate performance)
4. (felt generally comfortable; good performance)
5. (felt very comfortable; excellent performance)

Partner Rating of Comfort/Competency

Circle the number that best represents how well you feel your partner did in performing the role-play.

1. (he seemed very uncomfortable and unsure of himself)
2. (he appeared mildly uncomfortable and unsure of himself)
3. (he appeared fairly comfortable; adequate performance)
4. (he appeared generally comfortable; good performance)
5. (he appeared very comfortable; excellent performance)

Critical Components of Introducing Others

As there are important steps you should take when introducing yourself, there are also important steps to take when introducing someone else. These are:

1. Name the first person and tell him or her the name of the second person (e.g., "Bill, this is John Smith"). Speak clearly and loudly so that the names are heard by both people.
2. Name the second person and tell him or her the name of the first person (e.g., "John, this is Bill White").
3. Say something that helps the two people get to know each other (e.g., mention something they have in common; invite them to do something with you; say how you know each of them).

Practicing Introducing Others

Now you will participate in role-plays and practice introducing others. Some ideas for role-plays are introducing a new friend to other kids at school, introducing a new friend to your family, and introducing a sibling to your friends.

Remember to complete the Role-Play Recording Form.

Role-Play Recording Form

Date: ___________

Rehearsed skill: ______________________________

Role-play partner: ___________________________ (e.g., staff member, peer, parent, etc.)

Self-rating of Comfort/Competency

Circle the number that best represents how well you feel you did in performing the role-play.

1. (felt very uncomfortable and awkward)
2. (felt mildly uncomfortable and awkward)
3. (felt fairly comfortable; adequate performance)
4. (felt generally comfortable; good performance)
5. (felt very comfortable; excellent performance)

Partner rating of Comfort/Competency

Circle the number that best represents how well you feel your partner did in performing the role-play.

1. (he seemed very uncomfortable and unsure of himself)
2. (he appeared mildly uncomfortable and unsure of himself)
3. (he appeared fairly comfortable; adequate performance)
4. (he appeared generally comfortable; good performance)
5. (he appeared very comfortable; excellent performance)

Homework

✎ Practice introducing yourself and others. If you are in a residential treatment setting, you may practice with staff and/or other residents.

EXPRESSING GRATITUDE

Goals

- To understand the importance of expressing gratitude or being thankful
- To learn the critical components of expressing gratitude
- To practice expressing gratitude

Why Is Expressing Gratitude Important?

Expressing gratitude means to show someone that you are thankful. Gratitude means being grateful for, or appreciative of, what others have done for you. Being able to express gratitude to someone who has helped you is an important social skill. Good relationships are based on mutuality, or the reciprocal helping of one another, and saying "thank you" lets other people know that they are valued and their help is appreciated. In addition, saying "thank you" to a friend, parent, or teacher who has helped you in some way is a means of strengthening your connection or bond with that person, and it increases the chances that those people will be there for you when you need help in the future. If you do not express gratitude, the person who helped you may feel like you are taking advantage and that his or her actions are not appreciated. The person may end up thinking you are selfish and that you do not care about anyone's feelings but your own. These negative impressions may result in the person staying away from you and not offering you help or support the next time you need it.

Critical Components of Expressing Gratitude

Review the following steps for giving thanks.

1. Think about whether it might be appropriate to thank someone for helping you or showing kindness. It is especially important to thank people who helped you when they really didn't have to, or when they went out of their way to do something nice for you.
2. Pick the best time and place to express your gratitude (e.g., a quiet time, a private place, a place where you are sure you will have the other person's attention).
3. Consider different ways of thanking the person (e.g., words, a letter, a favor) and decide which way he or she would most appreciate.
4. Express your gratitude to that person. Be sure to tell the other person why you are thanking him or her. If giving thanks in person, look the person in the eyes and speak in a friendly and sincere manner.

Practicing Expressing Gratitude

Again, you will participate in role-plays in order to practice effective ways of expressing gratitude. Some ideas for role-plays are: 1) you are being bullied and someone steps in and stands up for you, 2) a classmate tutors you in a subject you are having trouble with, and 3) your sibling offers to do your chores so you can go out with your friends.

Remember to complete the Role-Play Recording Form.

Homework

✎ Practice giving thanks whenever someone does you a favor or does something nice for you.

Role-Play Recording Form

Date: ___________

Rehearsed skill: ______________________________

Role-play partner: ____________________________ (e.g., staff member, peer, parent, etc.)

Self-rating of Comfort/Competency

Circle the number that best represents how well you feel you did in performing the role-play.

1. (felt very uncomfortable and awkward)
2. (felt mildly uncomfortable and awkward)
3. (felt fairly comfortable; adequate performance)
4. (felt generally comfortable; good performance)
5. (felt very comfortable; excellent performance)

Partner Rating of Comfort/Competency

Circle the number that best represents how well you feel your partner did in performing the role-play.

1. (he seemed very uncomfortable and unsure of himself)
2. (he appeared mildly uncomfortable and unsure of himself)
3. (he appeared fairly comfortable; adequate performance)
4. (he appeared generally comfortable; good performance)
5. (he appeared very comfortable; excellent performance)

Goals

- To understand the importance of asking for help
- To learn the critical components of asking for help
- To practice asking for help

Why Is Asking for Help Important?

Everyone, at multiple points in his life, needs the help and support of others. Needing help is not a sign of weakness. In fact, it is the opposite. Being able to acknowledge that you need help and to reach out to others reflects self-confidence and the desire to be successful. There are many situations wherein a person would benefit from asking for help (e.g., not understanding a homework or job assignment).

Critical Components of Asking for Help

The following is a list of important steps in asking for help. Review them carefully.

1. Think about what you are struggling with. What is making it difficult to solve the problem? What effect is the problem having on you?
2. Decide if you need help with the problem. Is this something that you can easily solve by yourself, or would asking for help allow you to move on toward accomplishment of the goal or task?
3. Think about who could help you with the problem. Choose the best possible helper.
4. Approach the person and explain that you need his or her help. Be sure to fully describe the problem so that he or she will understand what you need. If the person is busy at the time, ask when you could come back and speak with him or her.

Practicing Asking for Help

Once more, you will participate in role-plays in order to practice asking for help. Some ideas for role-plays are asking a friend to help you study for a test, asking a teacher to explain how to solve a math problem, and asking a parent to help you practice job-interviewing skills.

Remember to complete the Role-Play Recording Form.

Homework

✎ Practice asking others for help, if the situation presents itself.

Role-Play Recording Form

Date: ___________

Rehearsed skill: ______________________________

Role-play partner: ____________________________ (e.g., staff member, peer, parent, etc.)

Self-rating of Comfort/Competency

Circle the number that best represents how well you feel you did in performing the role-play.

1. (felt very uncomfortable and awkward)
2. (felt mildly uncomfortable and awkward)
3. (felt fairly comfortable; adequate performance)
4. (felt generally comfortable; good performance)
5. (felt very comfortable; excellent performance)

Partner Rating of Comfort/Competency

Circle the number that best represents how well you feel your partner did in performing the role-play.

1. (he seemed very uncomfortable and unsure of himself)
2. (he appeared mildly uncomfortable and unsure of himself)
3. (he appeared fairly comfortable; adequate performance)
4. (he appeared generally comfortable; good performance)
5. (he appeared very comfortable; excellent performance)

APOLOGIZING

Goals

- To understand the importance of apologizing
- To learn the critical components of apologizing
- To practice apologizing

Why Is Apologizing Important?

It is important that a person be able to apologize when he makes a mistake or lets someone down. Everyone makes mistakes from time to time, but not everyone acknowledges his mistakes or apologizes for them. Being able to apologize shows others that you are able to admit your mistakes and that you are willing to make amends for wrongdoings.

Critical Components of Apologizing

Review the following steps for apologizing:

1. Think about what you did and how it may have affected the other person. Ask yourself if an apology would be appropriate (e.g., you broke something that belongs to someone else, you hurt someone's feelings, you lost your temper and cursed or hit someone).
2. Think about ways to apologize and pick the most appropriate. The most appropriate is not necessarily the easiest way to apologize—it is the way that would be most appreciated by the other person (e.g., say something, do something, write something).
3. Choose the best time and place to apologize.

4. Think about what you want to say. Make sure you acknowledge the mistake and its impact. Is there some way that you can make amends?

5. When apologizing, make good eye contact with the person you are talking to. Speak in a pleasant tone and in a loud enough voice for them to hear you. Be sincere. Act like you are apologizing not because you have to, but because you really want to.

Practicing Apologizing

You and the other members of your group will participate in role-plays wherein you practice apologizing for some wrongdoing or mistake. Possible role-plays include apologizing to a parent for staying out too late, apologizing to a friend for losing your temper and yelling at him, and apologizing to a teacher for acting up in class.

Remember to complete the Role-Play Recording Form.

Homework

✎ Identify someone whom you have hurt or let down during the past month and apologize to that person.

Role-Play Recording Form

Date: ___________

Rehearsed skill: ______________________________

Role-play partner: ____________________________ (e.g., staff member, peer, parent, etc.)

Self-rating of Comfort/Competency

Circle the number that best represents how well you feel you did in performing the role-play.

1. (felt very uncomfortable and awkward)
2. (felt mildly uncomfortable and awkward)
3. (felt fairly comfortable; adequate performance)
4. (felt generally comfortable; good performance)
5. (felt very comfortable; excellent performance)

Partner Rating of Comfort/Competency

Circle the number that best represents how well you feel your partner did in performing the role-play.

1. (he seemed very uncomfortable and unsure of himself)
2. (he appeared mildly uncomfortable and unsure of himself)
3. (he appeared fairly comfortable; adequate performance)
4. (he appeared generally comfortable; good performance)
5. (he appeared very comfortable; excellent performance)

Goals

- To understand the importance of recognizing your feelings
- To learn the critical components of recognizing your feelings
- To practice recognizing your feelings
- To begin using the Feelings Diary

Why is Recognizing Your Feelings Important?

Recognizing and identifying your feelings and emotions help you to better control and express yourself. For example, if you don't recognize emerging feelings of anger until others comment on the fact that you are yelling and look red in the face, then it can be embarrassing and contribute to the impression that you are out–of control. Alternatively, if you pick up on bodily sensations and thoughts that cue you to your emerging anger, then you have ample time to use coping skills and express yourself in a firm, but non-aggressive, manner. This is helpful not only for feelings of anger, but for other emotions, like sadness, as well.

Critical Components of Recognizing Your Feelings

Review the following steps:

1. Listen to your body. What sensations are you experiencing? Where are you experiencing them (e.g., butterflies in your stomach, tension in your hands and fists)? Have you felt this way before? Where were you and what was happening the last time you felt this way?
2. What just happened that triggered these feelings? Did someone say or do something to you? How did this affect you?

3. Pay attention to your thoughts. What are you thinking or saying to yourself about what just happened?

4. What would you call this feeling? Are there other feelings that you are having, as well? What do they feel like, and what would you call them? Do these feelings often occur together?

Practicing Recognizing Your Feelings

You and the other members of your group will practice recognizing feelings by participating in role-plays. Possible role-plays include: 1) your parents just told you that you are grounded for the weekend, and 2) you just failed a math test.

Remember to complete the Role-Play Recording Form.

Homework

✎ Monitor your feelings for the next week using the Feelings Diary on page 35. The diary should identify the feelings that you experienced, the situations in which they occurred, and the cues you used to recognize these feelings. You may photocopy the diary if necessary.

Role-Play Recording Form

Date: ___________

Rehearsed skill: ______________________________

Role-play partner: ____________________________ (e.g., staff member, peer, parent, etc.)

Self-rating of Comfort/Competency

Circle the number that best represents how well you feel you did in performing the role-play.

1. (felt very uncomfortable and awkward)
2. (felt mildly uncomfortable and awkward)
3. (felt fairly comfortable; adequate performance)
4. (felt generally comfortable; good performance)
5. (felt very comfortable; excellent performance)

Partner Rating of Comfort/Competency

Circle the number that best represents how well you feel your partner did in performing the role-play.

1. (he seemed very uncomfortable and unsure of himself)
2. (he appeared mildly uncomfortable and unsure of himself)
3. (he appeared fairly comfortable; adequate performance)
4. (he appeared generally comfortable; good performance)
5. (he appeared very comfortable; excellent performance)

Feelings Diary

Feeling	Situation	Cues
Anger	*My mother grounded me for not cleaning my bedroom like I said I would.*	*My face started to feel hot and my muscles got tight. I felt like I was going to cry.*

RECOGNIZING THE FEELINGS OF OTHERS

Goals

- To understand the importance of recognizing the feelings of others
- To learn the critical components of recognizing the feelings of others
- To practice recognizing the feelings of others

Why Is It Important to Recognize the Feelings of Others?

Being able to recognize how others are feeling is a skill that helps you to determine what behavior is appropriate and needed in a given social situation. For example, if you recognize that your friend or a family member is feeling anxious or depressed, you may be able to reach out and support him or her. Similarly, if you detect that someone is getting angry, then you may be able to defuse the situation and prevent an argument or fight from occurring.

Critical Components of Recognizing the Feelings of Others

Review the following steps:

1. Observe the other person's facial expression and body posture for cues. What do you see and what does it tell you? For example, are his muscles tense or relaxed? Does he seem to be seeking others out or pulling away? Have you seen him look or act that way before? What was going on with him the last time he looked that way?
2. Listen to his voice and words. Is he speaking calmly or does he seem excited or agitated? What is he saying? Is he asking for something from you or others?
3. If appropriate, reflect to the other person what you are seeing and hearing, and ask clarifying questions. For example, "You look really irritated; did something just happen to upset you?"

time you will not participate in role-plays, but, rather, you will take turns picking emotions out of a bowl or other container and expressing them *nonverbally*. This means you will have to rely on facial expressions and body gestures to express the particular emotion. As you attempt this, the other members of your group will try to guess your emotion or feeling.

Homework

✎ Observe one of your group members (you will pick his name out of a bowl during the meeting) over the course of the week. Pay attention to the emotions you observe and record them on the Observation Form provided on the next page.

Observation Form

Day/Date	Emotions Observed (note the person's facial and bodily expressions, words, and actions)

Goals

- To understand the importance of showing empathy
- To learn the critical components of showing empathy
- To practice showing empathy

Why Is Showing Empathy Important?

It is important that you are able to appropriately respond to others' expressed feelings and needs. This includes showing *empathy*, or an understanding of how someone feels in a given situation. You will learn more about empathy later on in the program (see Chapter 8). For now, you will learn the right way to go about showing someone that you empathize with him.

Critical Components of Showing Empathy

Review the following steps:

1. Think about what you see and hear, and make your best guess as to how the person might be feeling. Ask yourself how you would feel if you were in his situation.
2. Where appropriate (i.e., it wouldn't make the person even more upset or endanger your safety), reflect on what you have observed and ask the person if he would like to talk about it. If he says "no," then just let him know that you are sorry that he is upset and would be glad to talk with him later on, if he changes his mind.

3. If the other person indicates that he would like to talk, then comment on how you think he might be feeling and invite him to talk about his feelings (e.g., "You look really worried to me; I was wondering if there is something that you would like to talk about?").

4. Use your listening skills and allow the person to share how he is feeling. Ask him if there is something that you can do to help him. Where appropriate, express your regard for the person and reassure him that you will be there for him when he needs you.

Practicing Showing Empathy

You and the other members of your group will practice showing empathy by participating in role-plays. Possible role-plays include talking to a friend who just broke up with his girlfriend, talking to a friend who just got into an argument with his parents, and talking to your mother, who is feeling stressed out because you and your brother have both gotten into trouble at school.

Remember to complete the Role-Play Recording Form.

Homework

✎ Continue observing the person you picked last week (remember to complete the Observation Form. A copy is provided following the Role-Play Recording Form). Practice giving him support when you see that he needs help or someone to talk to.

Role-Play Recording Form

Date: __________

Rehearsed skill: ____________________________

Role-play partner: __________________________ (e.g., staff member, peer, parent, etc.)

Self-rating of Comfort/Competency

Circle the number that best represents how well you feel you did in performing the role-play.

1. (felt very uncomfortable and awkward)
2. (felt mildly uncomfortable and awkward)
3. (felt fairly comfortable; adequate performance)
4. (felt generally comfortable; good performance)
5. (felt very comfortable; excellent performance)

Partner Rating of Comfort/Competency

Circle the number that best represents how well you feel your partner did in performing the role-play.

1. (he seemed very uncomfortable and unsure of himself)
2. (he appeared mildly uncomfortable and unsure of himself)
3. (he appeared fairly comfortable; adequate performance)
4. (he appeared generally comfortable; good performance)
5. (he appeared very comfortable; excellent performance)

Observation Form

Day/Date	Emotions Observed (note the person's facial and body expressions, words, and actions)

ASKING SOMEONE FOR A DATE

Goals

- To understand the importance of asking someone for a date
- To learn the critical components of asking someone for a date
- To practice asking someone for a date

Importance of Asking Someone for a "Date"

Being able to ask someone out on a date is probably something you already think is important. Your therapist will talk to you briefly about why this skill can be helpful in reducing the risk of reoffending.

Critical Components of Asking Someone for a "Date"

Review the following steps of asking someone out:

1. Decide whom you would like to ask out. In making this decision, weigh the following factors: his or her age-appropriateness, evidence that he or she is interested in you, and whether you have things in common. Do you like the same things? Do you have compatible personalities?
2. Decide what situation would make for the easiest "first date." Typically, this is something that is not emotionally threatening and doesn't necessarily convey a romantic interest (e.g., eating lunch together, attending a ball game or after-school function, meeting at the mall, going bowling, etc.).
3. Decide the best time and place to ask the person out. Avoid asking the person in front of others or when he or she is busy or involved in some activity.

4. Approach the person in a friendly manner. Make good eye contact, smile and say "hello." Initially, make small talk. Observe whether the other person seems to be responding to you in a positive manner (i.e., making good eye contact, smiling back at you). If the conversation seems to be going well, proceed in asking the person to join you in the selected activity.

Practicing Asking Someone for a Date

You and the other members of your group will practice asking someone on a date by participating in role-plays with your therapist. Remember to complete the Role-Play Recording Form.

Role-Play Recording Form

Date: ___________

Rehearsed skill: ______________________________

Role-play partner: ____________________________ (e.g., staff member, peer, parent, etc.)

Self-rating of Comfort/Competency

Circle the number that best represents how well you feel you did in performing the role-play.

1. (felt very uncomfortable and awkward)
2. (felt mildly uncomfortable and awkward)
3. (felt fairly comfortable; adequate performance)
4. (felt generally comfortable; good performance)
5. (felt very comfortable; excellent performance)

Partner Rating of Comfort/Competency

Circle the number that best represents how well you feel your partner did in performing the role-play.

1. (he seemed very uncomfortable and unsure of himself)
2. (he appeared mildly uncomfortable and unsure of himself)
3. (he appeared fairly comfortable; adequate performance)
4. (he appeared generally comfortable; good performance)
5. (he appeared very comfortable; excellent performance)

Goals

- To understand the importance of handling rejection and disappointment
- To learn the critical components of handling rejection and disappointment
- To practice handling rejection and disappointment
- To complete the Social Skills Post-Test

Importance of Handling Rejection and Disappointment

Handling rejection and disappointment is both a coping skill and a social skill. It is normal and inevitable that you will be rejected and experience relationship disappointment at some point in your life. It happens to everyone, so you should not let it get to you. Just because someone turns you down does not mean you are inadequate. Also, one rejection does not mean that everyone will reject you and that you will forever be doomed to a life of loneliness. Interpersonal disappointment can occur in many contexts, including romantic relationships, friendships, family relationships, and work/business relationships. Therefore, accepting and learning to cope with these experiences is an important life skill.

Critical Components of Handling Rejection and Disappointment

Review the following steps:

1. Be mentally and emotionally prepared to handle the outcome—no matter what it may be. When getting ready to ask someone out for a date, remind yourself that he or she may decline the invitation.

2. When turned down, remind yourself that everybody has the right to decide whether or not to accept an invitation. While being rejected is not a pleasant experience, remember that it is not the "end of the world." Specifically, it does not necessarily mean that you did something wrong in how you approached the person or that he or she doesn't like you. Furthermore, it does not mean that everyone that you are potentially interested in will similarly reject you.
3. Be pleasant and gracious. While it is okay to show disappointment, don't look angry or make demeaning comments to the person. Instead, make it clear that you hope that the two of you can remain friends and will be able to do things together in the future.
4. If you really feel down about what happened, seek out a good friend or parent whom you can talk to. Getting support and processing feelings is a way of taking good care of yourself and ensuring that you will recover from your disappointment.
5. Be pleasant and friendly the next time you see the person. Don't harbor a grudge. Let it go and move on.

Practicing Handling Rejection and Disappointment

You and the other members of your group will practice handling rejection and disappointment by participating in role-plays. Possible role-plays being turned down for a date, not making the varsity sports team at school, and not getting a part in the school play.

Remember to complete the Role-Play Recording Form.

Role-Play Recording Form

Date: ___________

Rehearsed skill: ______________________________

Role-play partner: ____________________________ (e.g., staff member, peer, parent, etc.)

Self-rating of Comfort/Competency

Circle the number that best represents how well you feel you did in performing the role-play.

1. (felt very uncomfortable and awkward)
2. (felt mildly uncomfortable and awkward)
3. (felt fairly comfortable; adequate performance)
4. (felt generally comfortable; good performance)
5. (felt very comfortable; excellent performance)

Partner Rating of Comfort/Competency

Circle the number that best represents how well you feel your partner did in performing the role-play.

1. (he seemed very uncomfortable and unsure of himself)
2. (he appeared mildly uncomfortable and unsure of himself)
3. (he appeared fairly comfortable; adequate performance)
4. (he appeared generally comfortable; good performance)
5. (he appeared very comfortable; excellent performance)

Social Skills Post-Test

Just as you took a pre-test at the beginning of this module, you will be asked to complete a post-test at the end. Again, this is not like a test that you would take at school. Your therapist will use it to gauge your progress and determine whether you understand and comprehend the skills and techniques you have learned thus far. Your therapist will hand out copies of the test to you and the other members of the group.

Chapter 3 *Sexual Impulse Control and Judgment*

Introduction

In addition to having problems with social skills, the majority of adolescent males who engage in sexually abusive behavior have problems with impulse control and judgment. This means that you may tend to act first, and only later consider the consequences of your behavior. This module of treatment is designed to help you understand the personal, social, and legal consequences of acting impulsively. The main skill you will learn is how to "stop and think" before you act.

INTRODUCTION OF IMPULSE CONTROL AND JUDGMENT

Goals

- To learn the definition of key terms related to impulse control and judgment
- To understand the relationship between impulsivity and sexual offending behavior
- To complete the impulse control pre-test

Key Terms: Impulse, Impulse Control, Judgment, and Impulsivity

Impulse

What does it mean to have an impulse? An impulse is an urge or desire to do something. People experience impulses or urges as something they *want* or *need* at given moments in time. Urges are usually associated with various biological states or states of mind. For example, when you are hungry, you experience the urge to eat, and when you are thirsty, you experience the urge to drink. If you are angry, you may experience an urge to scream at someone or even hit him. In this same way, people sometimes experience various sexual urges or desires.

It is important to understand that it is normal to experience a variety of impulses, including certain sexual urges. Urges alert us to certain basic needs, such as eating, drinking, and sleeping. If we didn't ever satisfy these basic needs, we would die. Sexual urges, however, are not essential to life. You will not die if you do not have sex. Sexual urges can be strong, though, and they can have a powerful influence on your behavior.

Impulse Control

Learning how and when to control your urges or impulses is called *impulse control.* Although you have little control over the types of urges you experience, you do have control over the decision-making process in which you decide whether to try and satisfy your urge at that given moment. Lots of things need to be considered in deciding whether or not to give in to an urge. Ask yourself:

- Is this an urge that might hurt someone (or me) if I choose to express it?
- Is this the right time and place to express it?
- Is there something else that I should be doing now, instead of giving in to this urge?
- What is likely to happen if I act on this urge at this time, and with this person?
- Will I get in trouble if I act in this way?

Judgment

Judgment is the inner process of asking questions and considering the potential consequences of acting on an urge. It is the cognitive, decision-making process that helps guide your behavior when you are driven to satisfy an urge. In essence, it tells you whether some desired action should be taken or not taken, based on a number of important considerations. Of course, your judgment may be good or bad, and sometimes people go ahead and do something anyway, even though they know it is wrong or harmful. Things like age, maturity level, and intelligence are some factors that may influence a person's decision to act on urges or impulses. Good judgment comes from taking the time to stop and think about the potential consequences of your actions. If you act in a hasty manner, and don't think things through, you cannot make good judgments.

Impulsivity

What does it mean to be impulsive? Being *impulsive* means to act or do things without really taking the time to think through the situation. People can act impulsively in a variety of different ways, with a variety of consequences. Impulsivity can lead to problems with weight control, drinking, substance abuse, etc. It can also lead to criminal behavior.

Sexual Behavior, Impulse Control, and Judgment

In group, your therapist will discuss with you and the other members the relationship between impulsivity and sexual offending behavior. Many adolescents who sexually offend have impulse-control problems. It is important to understand that there is a relationship between impulsivity and mood. For example, if you were angry at your parents and jealous of your siblings, this could interfere with your ability to exercise good impulse control and judgment.

This treatment module focuses on teaching you how to "stop and think" before acting on a sexual urge or impulse. You will be taught a technique that you can use in your everyday life that will improve your sexual impulse control and judgment. Mastery of impulse control can lower your risk of sexually re-offending.

Impulse Control Pre-Test

Just as you did at the beginning of the previous module on social skills, you will take a pre-test at the start of this module on impulse control. Again, this is not like a test you would take at school. This test will not be graded. It is designed to evaluate your understanding of the skills you are being taught in this program.

Your therapist will hand out copies of the impulse control pre-test to you and the other members of the group. He or she will collect them and review the results with you at your next meeting. These tests will help you and your therapist set your treatment goals.

Homework

✎ Complete the Impulse Control Pre-Test.

PRE-TEST RESULTS AND TREATMENT GOALS

Goal

- To go over your pre-test results and set goals for treatment

My Treatment Goals

Together with your therapist, use the space provided to develop your treatment goals and list them in order of importance.

My Treatment Goals—Impulse Control Module

1. ____
2. ____
3. ____
4. ____
5. ____

Homework

✎ Review your goals with your therapist and bring them to your next meeting.

THE "STOP AND THINK" PROCEDURE

Goals

- To learn and practice the "Stop and Think" procedure
- To complete the Impulse Control Post-Test

Overview

The "Stop and Think" procedure is designed to:

1. increase your understanding of the thoughts, feelings, and events that led to your offending behavior,
2. increase your understanding of your particular, offense-specific sexual thoughts and behaviors,
3. provide practice in interrupting inappropriate sexual thoughts before they lead to heightened sexual arousal and offending behavior,

3\. help you learn to avoid high-risk behaviors, and

4\. help you become better aware of, and vicariously experience, the rewards of practicing good sexual impulse control and judgment.

The Steps to "Stop and Think"

The "Stop and Think" procedure is composed of several steps, which are outlined in the sections that follow.

Step 1: Neutral

The first step of the "Stop and Think" procedure is called the *neutral* step. This step requires you to take 20–0 seconds to think about where you were, what you were doing, and how you were feeling *before* you had any specific sexual thoughts. For example, *"I see myself sitting at home on the sofa watching TV. Nothing much is going on and I'm feeling kind of bored and restless. None of my friends are around and I am looking for something to do."*

Thinking about the thoughts, feelings, and behaviors that occurred before you committed the offense (the *antecedents*) will help you begin to understand how they are linked to your sexual behavior. You may feel that you "don't know" why you did what you did, just that you were driven to do it, and this is where the "Stop and Think" procedure can help.

Step 2: Sexual Thoughts

The *sexual thoughts* step consists of the thoughts you had that led up to the sexual offense. During this step, you will describe the thoughts you had regarding planning the sexual offense. You also will describe the emotions you felt at the time, including your level of sexual arousal. You will *not* describe the offense itself. For example, your parents leave you home alone to babysit your younger sister. You invite her up your room to watch a movie. As you walk into your bedroom, you think to yourself, *"I am nervous, but excited at the same time. As I am looking at my sister and thinking about what I can get her to do, I am getting more and more turned-on."*

This step of the procedure should also include descriptions of other relevant motives for your behavior, such as anger or feelings of rejection, and stimulus events, such as the viewing of pornography. This step should take approximately 2–3 minutes to complete. As you practice the "stop and think" technique, this step will take less time. The idea is for this step to help you identify risky thoughts and circumstances so that you can learn to stop or interrupt them.

Step 3: Consequences

The next step in the procedure is imagining the negative *consequences* of having sexually acted-out. This should include description of the things that actually did happen to you and your family. It can also include things that might have happened or could happen if you were to reengage in this behavior (e.g., going to jail, being removed from your home, being sued, etc.) The point here is to explore the negative impact your offense had on your life and the lives of those close to you. For example, *"I am sitting in court and looking up at the judge. He has a mean look on his face. This is the first time I have ever been in trouble like this and I am feeling scared and anxious. The judge says, 'I am going to send you to juvenile corrections until your 18th birthday.'"*

Step 4: Second Neutral

Step 4 is called the *second neutral.* This is either a repetition of your first neutral scene (see Step 1) or a completely new neutral scene (if you committed more than one sexual offense). Completing a second neutral scene provides you with insight into the situations and thinking patterns that lead to your sexual acting-out. It also provides you with the opportunity to continue practicing interrupting your problematic sexual thoughts.

Step 5: Second Sexual Thoughts

Consistent with the previous step, Step 5 requires you to either repeat your description of the events and thoughts that led up to the sexual offense or to describe the events and thoughts that led up to a different sexual offense (if you committed more than one). Again, it is important to note that we do not want you to describe the actual offense; just the thoughts and events that led up to it.

Step 6: Second Consequences

Here, we once again want you to imagine the negative consequences of your behavior. Try to come up with different consequences than you did in Step 3.

Step 7: Escape

The *escape* step is an important component of the stop-and-think procedure. In this step, you imagine a different outcome, one that is positive and in which you do not commit the sexual offense. This step helps you imagine the rewards of exercising good sexual judgment and impulse control.

To complete this step, describe a scene in which you avoid a high-risk situation. For example, your parents ask you to babysit your younger sibling while they go grocery shopping. You recognize this as a risky situation, so you say, *"Hey Mom, you remember when I was in treatment they told me not to be alone with a younger child; that it wasn't a good idea? Maybe we should just all go to the store together; that way I can help you and Dad."*

Practicing "Stop and Think"

Together as a group, and with guidance from your therapist, you and your peers will practice the stop-and-think procedure in session.

When practicing the technique, it is important that you speak in the first person (e.g., "I see myself ...) and in the present tense (e.g., "I am sitting in the living room ... ") You should also try to be as detailed as possible, providing insight into your internal bodily sensations, as well as your mood and state of mind.

At first, this procedure can be difficult to complete. The Stop and Think Worksheet provided will help you to organize your thoughts so you can successfully practice the procedure. Remember to use the first person in the present tense. Your therapist may instruct you to record yourself practicing the procedure out loud. Or, you may be instructed to practice the procedure with your therapist or other staff member in private.

Stop and Think Worksheet

Step 1: Neutral

Step 2: Sexual Thoughts

Step 3: Consequences

Step 4: Second Neutral

Step 5: Second Sexual Thoughts

Step 6: Second Consequences

Step 7: Escape

Impulse Control Post-Test

At the completion of the module, your therapist will once again administer a post-test. Like the one you took in the last module, this test will help your therapist gauge your progress and determine whether you understand and comprehend the skills you learned thus far.

Chapter 4 *Healthy Masculinity I*

Introduction

Many youths who have committed sexual offenses have been exposed to male aggression or antisocial behavior at some point in their lives. Exposure to violence can lead to distorted views of manhood and rigid beliefs about how men should address conflict and respond to various life challenges. The Healthy Masculinity component of treatment is designed to offer you an alternative view of masculinity.

EXPLORING IMAGES OF MASCULINITY

Goals

- To talk about how society typically defines "being a man"
- To explore developmental influences on masculine identity
- To discuss popular images of males in our society
- To complete the Healthy Masculinity I Pre-Test

What it Means to "Be a Man"

In group, you will discuss how our society has traditionally defined masculinity. Some characteristics that are associated with being "male" are:

- "strong"
- "tough" (i.e. "can take it"; doesn't cry, etc.)

- can handle problems by himself
- controls expression of feelings
- defends self and family/friends
- sexual prowess and readiness from a young age
- responsible and protects and takes care of others

See if you can come up with some others and list them here:

- ______________________________
- ______________________________
- ______________________________

Think about these characteristics and identify what is good and bad about each of them. For example, when does being "tough" help you, and when does it not? Sometimes being tough makes it easier to deal with hardships. On the other hand, it can make it hard to recognize and resolve problems.

Do you think society's definition of masculinity has changed over the years? If so, how has it changed and what are some of the forces behind these changes? Discuss your thoughts with the group.

Developmental Influences

This topic focuses on the question, "Where do we learn about being a male?" Identify the major male influences in your life (both positive and negative), and list them in the space provided. Be sure to include parents, older siblings, older boys in school or in the neighborhood, etc. Write down what you learned from each of these people. Were these things useful or harmful?

Men in My Life	What They Taught Me
1. ______________	______________
2. ______________	______________
3. ______________	______________
4. ______________	______________
5. ______________	______________

Popular Images of Males

In group, you will explore both positive and negative, or stereotypic, images of males as depicted in the media. Your therapist may have you review lyrics and listen to songs from popular artists that depict positive messages and images of males. If you participate in this activity, you may want to ask yourself the following questions about the particular song or lyrics:

- What is the message the artist is trying to communicate?
- Why do you think he chose to record that song?
- Why do some artists put out recordings that glorify sexual aggression and violence?

You will also discuss male images in television, movies, and video games. Your therapist will ask you to identify positive and negative examples from each of these media and explain what makes each one good or bad.

Healthy Masculinity I Pre-Test

Your therapist will hand out copies of the Healthy Masculinity Pre-Test to you and the other members of the group. He or she will collect them and review the results with you at your next meeting. These tests will help you and your therapist set your treatment goals.

Homework

✎ Complete the Healthy Masculinity I Pre-Test.

PRE-TEST RESULTS AND TREATMENT GOALS

Goal

- To go over your pre-test results and set goals for treatment

My Treatment Goals

Together with your therapist, use the space provided to develop your treatment goals and list them in order of importance.

My Treatment Goals—Healthy Masculinity I Module

1. ____
2. ____
3. ____
4. ____
5. ____

Homework

✎ Review your goals with your therapist and bring them to your next meeting.

CHILDHOOD EXPOSURE TO VIOLENCE AND ITS EFFECTS

Goal

- To explore the effects of childhood exposure to violence

Effects of Childhood Exposure to Violence

In preparation for a group discussion of the effects of being exposed to violence as a child, review the following facts. Your therapist will elaborate on them in session.

- It is estimated that by age 18 an American child will have viewed 16,000 simulated murders and 200,000 acts of violence.
- Boys spend an average of 13 hours a week playing video games; the majority of these games contain violence.

- Playing a lot of video games is related to having more aggressive thoughts, feelings, and behavior.
- Youths who viewed lots of violence on TV were more likely to be arrested and prosecuted for criminal acts as an adult.

Think about your own childhood and identify any experiences when you were exposed to violence. How did these experiences influence you? What did you learn about males and masculinity from these experiences?

THE CYCLE OF VIOLENCE

Goals

- To learn about the cycle of violence
- To discuss the steps in the cycle of violence

Introduction to the Cycle of Violence

It is very important to understand that interpersonal violence is a major problem in our society and that men account for the majority of the sexual and physical assaults against other men, women, and children. Review the following facts:

- 90% of murders committed in the United States in 2002 were perpetrated by males; more than 71% of the incidents involved a firearm.
- Males account for approximately 86% of all violent offenders.
- From 1992 to 1996, victimization by an intimate (i.e., spousal violence) accounted for about 21% of the violence experienced by females.
- About 30% of female murder victims were killed by a spouse, ex-spouse, or boyfriend.

- Children are exposed to this violence. Slightly more than one-half of female victims of intimate violence live in households with children under the age of 12.
- Males account for about 99% of the sexual assaults of adults and 94% of the sexual assaults of juveniles. More than one-third of the perpetrators of juvenile assaults were family members.

Committing acts of violence often leads to legal consequences for the perpetrator. Take a look at the following facts and discuss with the group why you think men in jail exhibit these characteristics:

- 60% of prison inmates (male and female) in 2002 were racial or ethnic minorities.
- More than one-half of inmates grew up in a single-parent household or with a guardian.
- Nearly one-fifth of inmates had a father, and one-third had a brother, who had been incarcerated.

Discuss with the group how early childhood exposure to violence, the absence of healthy male models, the effects of poverty, the lack of economic and educational opportunities, and racism can lead to violent behavior.

Book Discussion

As part of this session, your therapist may engage you and your peers in a group reading activity. Your therapist will choose a book that explores the theme of violence in young males and ask you to read and discuss certain parts.

Steps in the Cycle of Violence

Review the following steps of the cycle of violence (from Nathan McCall's book, *Makes Me Wanna Holler*) and apply the cycle to your own life.

Step 1. "Childhood optimism" (very young children typically have a naive innocence and optimism about life and the inherent "goodness" of people)

Step 2. "Disillusionment" (e.g., death or incarceration of father; seeing mother abused; child abuse, etc.)

Step 3. "Anger" (life is viewed as unfair and people are seen as exploitive and untrustworthy; survival is being stronger than others and taking what you want or need)

Step 3. "Violence" (often a response to a sense of injustice and an attempt to get back at others)

Step 4. "Death or imprisonment" (i.e., a life of violence is usually short-lived).

THE IMPORTANCE OF POSITIVE FATHERING AND MALE MENTORING

Goal

- To learn about and discuss healthy male role-modeling

Healthy Male Role-Modeling

It is very important for young men to have healthy male role models to look to for advice and encouragement. Having a positive role model can help you cope with the pressures of growing up. A good male role model can provide you with a strong sense of what is right and what is wrong, teach you how to resolve conflicts without resorting to violence, help you develop self-confidence so you don't feel the need to prove yourself to others, and instill in you a sense of self-respect as well as respect for others.

Think about the major male influences in your life (refer back to the list you made earlier) and identify those who have had a positive impact on your life. These are your healthy male role models.

Book or Movie Discussion

As before, your therapist may engage you and your peers in a group reading activity. Or, your therapist may show a movie with a theme of male relationships, particularly the father-son relationship. Think about your relationship with your own father. What kind of father do you want to be? Do you even want to be a father? Discuss your thoughts with the group.

REDEMPTION

Goal

- To explore the role of redemption in overcoming personal problems

Redemption

In group, you will discuss redemption and its relationship to sexual offending. Your therapist may ask you the following questions:

- What does redemption (i.e., recovery; overcoming a problem and redeeming oneself) mean?
- How does redemption relate to "Healthy Masculinity"
- Did the author/character/director (of the book or movie you have been discussing in group) seek redemption in his life?
- What is the link between redemption and hope?
- How does redemption relate to treatment for sexual behavior problems?

Goal

- To discuss the consequences of being intolerant and emotionally rigid, particularly when it comes to your views on what it means to be a man

Intolerance and Emotional Rigidity

This part of the Healthy Masculinity module is designed to help you develop a balanced sense of masculine identity. It is important to understand that not all men "need" to be "manly." Men can communicate their emotional needs and develop supportive and rewarding relationships with others. This does not make them "weak" or "feminine." Rigid thinking about what it means to be a "man" can lead to emotional isolation and bigotry. It can also lead to a lack of tolerance of differences in the way some men express themselves, as well as an unfounded prejudice against homosexuals. In group, your therapist will work with you to correct some of the common misunderstandings and fears you may have about homosexuality.

You will also discuss the consequences of not properly and effectively expressing your emotions, including:

- Repressed feelings,
- Emotional and social isolation/loneliness,
- Overdependency on females for emotional support, and
- Lashing out at others because they are different based on race, religion, or sexual orientation.

Think about your history and the level of tolerance you have shown for others who are different from you. If your tolerance level is low, think about whether this is this something that has negatively impacted your relationships and inner sense of happiness.

UNHEALTHY RELATIONSHIPS WITH FEMALES

Goals

- To discuss how rigid beliefs about masculinity can negatively affect male-female relationships
- To complete the Healthy Masculinity I Post-Test

Male-Female Relationships

Rigid traditional beliefs about masculinity and male-female roles can lead to relationship dysfunction and abuse. You will discuss with the group traditional relationships between males and females. What was the male's role versus the female's role in these relationships? (For example, males should be dominant and females submissive, men should work and women should stay home, etc.) What beliefs was this role definition based on? Discuss problems that have emerged from these expectations, especially when they are too rigid. Consider the following issues, both in general and in terms of your own life experiences:

- men having strained relationships with their wives
- men not really knowing their children or being there for them when them when they were needed
- physical and emotional abuse of women and children

Healthy Masculinity I Post-Test

At the completion of the module, your therapist will once again administer a post-test to gauge your progress and determine whether or not you are ready to move on to the next phase of treatment. You therapist will hand out copies of the test in group.

Phase II

Chapter 5 *Anger Management*

Introduction

Anger is a universal emotion—everyone experiences it from time to time and many people, at least at some point in their lives, have had difficulty successfully managing it. Some people lose control of their anger and get into fights (verbal or physical). Others keep their angry feelings inside because they do not want to embarrass themselves or lose control. Either way, managing your anger inappropriately can lead to problems.

The anger-management module of treatment will help you learn to recognize your anger before it causes harm to you or to others and to express your angry feelings in a healthy way.

THE IMPORTANCE OF CONTROLLING ANGER

Goals

- To discuss the inevitability of frustration and anger
- To identify and discuss poor ways of responding to frustration and anger
- To reflect on anger in your own life
- To complete the Anger Management Pre-Test

The Inevitability of Frustration and Anger

Everyone becomes irritated, frustrated, or angry from time to time. Think about your own life, and identify some events that can cause you to become angry. Using the space provided, begin your list with mildly stressful or irritating events and end with those that are highly stressful or provocative. Some examples of mild to moderately irritating events include:

- a teacher gives an extra-long homework assignment
- you misplace one of your belongings (e.g., glasses)
- you "flub-up" in a game (e.g., drop a pass or throw the ball to the other team)
- a youth at school makes a cutting or sarcastic comment to you

Examples of moderately to highly stressful or provocative events:

- someone pushes in front of you in the lunch line
- your parents ground you for the weekend
- you do poorly on a test even though you studied very hard
- another youth tries to pick a fight with you by pushing or hitting you

My Anger Situations

1. ____
2. ____
3. ____
4. ____
5. ____

It is impossible to totally avoid stress and frustration as you go through your daily life. This is what we mean when we say frustration and anger are *inevitable*: they cannot be avoided. You have little or no control over external events, including the actions of others. Instead, what you always can control is how you view (interpret) and respond to stressful events.

In this module on anger management, you will work with your therapist to learn to recognize, interpret, and respond to anger and frustration in positive ways.

Maladaptive Ways of Responding to Frustration

There are good and bad ways of dealing with anger and frustration. Bad or *maladaptive* ways include:

- screaming at someone or cursing
- threatening someone with bodily harm
- invading someone's physical space in an intimidating way
- hitting or physically attacking someone

Less directly aggressive, but still nonproductive, ways of responding to irritation or anger include sarcasm or refusing to do what someone has asked. It is important to understand that if you respond aggressively to an irritating situation, others involved may become aggressive as well. This can lead to arguments, physical fights, and, in extreme cases, legal consequences (e.g., being arrested). Such behavior may also result in personal or social consequences, such as losing a job or being suspended from school. Passive-aggressive responses, such as sarcasm, can damage friendships or relationships with family members. Even passive responses, such as silence and withdrawal, can have consequences. These include an increase in stress and tension, and feelings of inadequacy.

Reflecting on Your Anger

Identify three times in your life when you failed to properly handle your anger or frustration. Use the worksheet provided to describe how you handled the situation at the time and what the consequences were for yourself and others. Finally, describe how you would have liked to have handled this situation, and why.

Anger Reflection Worksheet

Situation	What I Did	Consequences	What I Should Have Done and Why

Anger Management Pre-Test

Your therapist will hand out copies of the Anger Management Pre-Test to you and the other members of the group. He or she will collect them and review the results with you at your next meeting. These tests will help you and your therapist set your treatment goals.

Homework

✎ Complete the Anger Management Pre-Test.

PRE-TEST RESULTS AND TREATMENT GOALS

Goal

- To go over your pre-test results and set goals for treatment

My Treatment Goals

Together with your therapist, use the worksheet provided to develop your treatment goals and list them in order of importance.

My Treatment Goals—Anger Management Module

1. ____

2. ____

3. ____

4. ____

5. ____

Homework

✎ Review your goals with your therapist and bring them to your next meeting.

THE ROLE OF ANGER IN SEXUAL OFFENDING

Goal

- To explore the role of anger in sexual offending

The Role of Anger in Sexual Offending

How can anger lead to sexual offending? Anger can make it easier to hurt someone, and it can make you less concerned about the consequences of your actions. Anger can lead to an "I don't care" attitude.

Together with your therapist, your group will identify situations or circumstances that can generate anger that can lead to sexual acting out with a child. Examples include:

- Feeling jealous or resentful of a younger sibling because you think your parents give him or her special treatment
- Feeling angry because your parents always ask you to take care of your younger sibling
- Feeling angry or mistreated because you were once victimized

Of course, anger can also lead to sexual acting out with peers and adults. Some youths use sex as a way of getting back at (or humiliating) someone they don't like or with whom they are angry.

ANGER MANAGEMENT STEPS

Goals

- To learn the steps of effective anger management
- To begin using the Anger Diary
- To develop an Anger Hierarchy

Steps to Anger Management

There are 5 steps to effective anger management:

1. Recognize signs of anger
2. Effectively use coping skills, including breathing and relaxation exercises
3. Identify and change faulty thinking that increases anger
4. Express yourself in an assertive but controlled manner
5. Resolve conflict through negotiation and compromise

Each of these steps will be a focus of one or more group therapy sessions.

Development of an Anger Diary

At this point in treatment, your therapist will introduce the Anger Diary. Initially, you will use the diary to record daily episodes of anger and the events or situations that triggered them. Ultimately, it should also include the recording of anger-related thoughts and the coping skills you used to deal with them (you will learn more about this later on in the chapter). You should complete an Anger Diary daily and bring it with you to group (a blank copy for your use is provided at the end of the chapter).

Development of an Anger Hierarchy

You will also begin using an Anger Hierarchy (a blank copy for your use is provided at the end of the chapter). This form will help you identify external triggers of anger. Events are ranked from 0 to 100 based on how stressful they are, and how likely they are to evoke anger. Items ranked at 25 are those that are mildly stressful. In other words, they are irritating but generally manageable. Items ranked at 50 are moderately stressful. They clearly evoke anger but don't always result in loss of control. Items ranked at 75 or higher are experienced as very stressful and typically result in loss of behavioral control (such as cursing at someone, destroying property, or getting physical).

Homework

✎ Complete the Anger Diary on page 100 and make daily entries (you may make photocopies if necessary). At this time, you need only record daily episodes of anger and the events or situations that triggered them (the first two columns of the form).

✎ Complete the initial part of the Anger Hierarchy on page 101 (list stressful situations only at this point). Identify events at three points on the rating scale: stress levels of 25, 50, and 75.

STEP 1: LEARNING TO RECOGNIZE ANGER

Goal

- To learn to recognize the warning signs of anger

Today you will be introduced to the idea of "cues" or warning signs of anger (Step 1 of anger management). Cues may be both *internal* and *external.* Internal cues are those that you directly experience in the form of a bodily sensation or feeling. For example, your heart may begin to beat harder when you get angry or tense. Other examples of internal cues include:

- Muscle tension (e.g.,face, neck, chest)
- "Butterflies" in your stomach
- Sweating
- Increased breathing rate
- Clenching your teeth

Can you think of any others?

- ______________________
- ______________________
- ______________________
- ______________________
- ______________________

There also may be external signs of anger that other people may notice. Examples include:

- narrowing your eyes
- staring in a menacing way
- getting red in the face
- speaking in a loud voice
- baring your teeth
- making intimidating gestures

External signs may also include ways others react to you when you are angry or acting in an aggressive manner. Some examples include:

- others begin to back away from you or avoid eye contact with you

- others get quiet when you speak
- others start to show signs of becoming angry in response to your demonstrated anger (e.g., they start speaking more loudly, they get red in the face, etc.)

Early detection of emerging feelings of anger is very important. Anger is like sexual arousal in that the longer you remain in the state, the more intense the feelings become, and the more difficult they are to control.

Homework

✎ Continue using the Anger Diary and begin recording your anger warning signs (Column 3 of the form).

✎ Add anger cues to your Anger Hierarchy entries.

STEP 2: CONTROLLING YOUR EMOTIONS

Goal

- To learn different techniques for calming yourself when angry

Introduction of Calming Techniques

Today you will be taught four techniques for calming yourself when angry or upset:

1. progressive muscle relaxation (PMR)
2. cue-controlled relaxation
3. breathing-cued relaxation
4. relaxing without tension

Mastery of these techniques will make it easier for you to exercise good judgment and impulse control. Mastering skills to control your emotions is Step 2 of successful anger management; Step 1 is being able to recognize your warning signs of anger.

Progressive Muscle Relaxation

The first and most fundamental of the anger-reduction techniques you will learn is *progressive muscle relaxation* (PMR). Mastery of PMR is critical because all of the other techniques you will learn are built upon it.

Progressive muscle relaxation teaches you to relax your muscles through a two-step process. First, you deliberately apply tension to certain muscle groups, and then you stop the tension and turn your attention to noticing how the muscles relax as the tension flows away. You may use the following sample script to practice PMR. You may wish to record yourself reciting the script so that you can play the recording any time you wish to practice the technique.

Sample PMR Script

Slowly tighten your right fist. Feel the tension in your hand and how it begins to radiate up your arm. Hold the tension in your fist for five seconds, then let go. Let's count together… 1… 2… 3… 4… and 5—let go. Drop your hand to your lap. Good. Notice how your hand feels as the tension is released and your hand relaxes. Think about how much better you feel when you let go of muscle tension; imagine the tension flowing out of your hand and relaxation flowing in as we go through this exercise. S stay relaxed for about twenty seconds.

(Pause for 20 seconds).

Now, slowly tighten your right fist again. Once again, concentrate on the difference in how your muscles feel when they are tensed instead of relaxed. Hold the tension for about five seconds, then let it go. Let's count out-loud again--1…2…3…4…5—let go. Let the tension flow out and the relaxation flow in.

(Pause for 20 seconds.)

(Repeat the described procedure with the left hand)

Now let's work on your right bicep. That's the muscle up here in your arm Tighten it as you curl up your arm. Again, we are going to hold it for about five seconds ... 1... 2... 3... 4... and 5—and now let go. Let your arm drop to your lap or the arm of the chair and concentrate on how much better it feels when you are relaxed instead of tense. Let's wait a few more seconds and then do the same thing again.

(Pause for 20 seconds)

Tighten-up your right bicep and hold it for five seconds... 1... 2... 3 ...4 ... and 5 —let go. Very good. Just concentrate on letting go of tension and letting warmth and relaxation set in.

(Pause for 20 seconds. Repeat the described procedure with the left bicep.)

Now we are going to turn to the chest. By squeezing your shoulder blades together, you are going to tighten the muscles in your chest. Everybody try it. Tighten-up your chest and hold the tension for about five seconds... 1... 2... 3... 4... and 5—let go. Feel the tension flow out and the relaxation set in. Stay relaxed for about 20 seconds. (Pause for 20 seconds.)

Now let's tighten the chest muscles once again. Feel the tension ... 1... 2... 3... 4...and 5—let go. Now you should feel relaxed in your arms and in your chest. Imagine the relaxation slowly spreading throughout your body—pretty soon you are going to feel relaxed throughout your whole body.

(Pause for 20 seconds.)

Now let's move up to the neck. The neck muscles often hold tension when we feel stressed, so it is very important that we learn to properly relax them. Sit in your chair so that the back of your head is pressed up against the wall behind you. Press your head against the wall so that you can feel tension in your neck muscles. Hold the tension for about five seconds. Let's count together...... 1... 2... 3... 4... and 5. Release and relax your neck. Feel the tension slowly go away. Good. Now, stay relaxed for about 20 seconds—just concentrate on how good it feels to be relaxed.

(Pause for 20 seconds.)

Now we are going to repeat the exercise. Press your head against the wall and hold the tension for about five seconds... 1... 2... 3... 4... and 5. Good, relax your neck and let the tension slowly go away. Concentrate on how good it feels to release tension and let relaxation set in.

(Pause for 20 seconds.)

Next we are going to concentrate on the muscles in our face. I want you to tightly close your eyes and scrunch-up your face. Good. Now hold the tension for about five seconds...1... 2... 3... 4... and 5. Let go of the tension. Let the muscles in your face relax. Let's stay with the relaxation for about 20 seconds.

(Pause for 20 seconds.)

Now, lets do it again. Tightly close your eyes and scrunch-up your face. 1... 2... 3... 4... and 5. Let the tension go and relax your face. Very good.

(Pause for 20 seconds.)

Now let's move to our legs. I want you to lift your right leg up so that it is parallel to the floor. Watch me. Lift your leg up and hold the tension... 1... 2... 3... 4... and 5. Put your leg down and relax for about twenty seconds.

(Pause for 20 seconds.)

Now let's do it again. Lift your leg up and hold the tension... 1... 2... 3... 4... and 5. Place your leg back on the floor and release the tension. Stay relaxed for about twenty seconds.

(Pause for 20 seconds. Repeat the described procedure with the left leg.)

Now your whole body should feel nice and relaxed. Think about each of the muscles we just relaxed. They should all feel heavy and warm. It you detect tension anywhere in your body. Re-do the exercise for that muscle group. I'm going to give you a couple of minutes to check for tension in your body and re-do the relaxation exercises for any muscles that still feel tense.

(Pause 2 minutes.).

Now I want everybody to close their eyes and take a deep breath and hold it. 1...2...3...relax. Let your breath out slowly. As you exhale, imagine all the tension flowing out of your body and relaxation setting in. Let's do it again. 1...2...3... exhale slowly. Concentrate on how good it feels to be relaxed. Let's take a deep breath and hold it one more time. 1...2...3...relax. Keep your eyes closed and concentrate on staying relaxed.

Cue-Controlled Relaxation

Cue-controlled relaxation involves identifying a word or phrase that will remind you to relax when you are feeling stressed. Come up with a word or phrase that you would like to use. Make sure that the word or phrase is easy to remember. For example, you may say to yourself "chill out" or "relax" if you find yourself starting to get angry while talking to someone else (e.g., your teacher, your parent, your friend). The word or phrase thus serves as a cue or reminder that maintaining self-composure is important during times of strife, and that you have the capacity (and responsibility) to stay calm no matter what the other person says or does.

For maximum effectiveness, the word or phrase you choose should be associated with a psychological state of tranquility and well-being. To accomplish this, you can imagine the word or phrase as you are *exhaling* during the PMR exercise.

Breathing-Cued Relaxation

Breathing-cued relaxation involves learning to progressively relax your body and mind with each slow exhale after a deep breath. The ability to do this is enhanced by your previous practice of deep breathing following PMR. This type of relaxation reduces the time you need to relax – down to a couple of minutes in most cases.

Relaxation Without Tension

This technique involves the release of muscle tension without the tensing of the muscles. Unlike in PMR, where you tense the muscles first, here you will simply concentrate on relaxing your various muscle groups. For example, think about your face and try to relax it; don't scrunch it up first. Mastering this type of relaxation takes time and practice. If you have successfully mastered the other techniques, however, you should be able to master this one pretty easily.

Homework

- ✎ Practice relaxation techniques and record on the Relaxation Practice Log when you practiced and how helpful it was.
- ✎ Continue to make daily entries in the Anger Diary (Columns 1–3).
- ✎ List relaxation techniques as coping skills on your Anger Hierarchy.

Relaxation Practice Log

Day/Time	Technique	How did you feel?

Goals

- To learn a technique called cognitive restructuring that will help you recognize and replace negative thoughts
- To learn the different types of negative thoughts
- To practice replacing negative thoughts with coping statements

Recognizing and Replacing Negative Thoughts

The way in which you perceive and interpret situations can make a big difference in how you consequently feel about and react to them. For example, you may believe that not defending yourself when someone says something negative about you will make you look "weak" and cause others to lose respect for you. When something like this happens, you probably feel a great deal of pressure to "set the record straight" or get back at the person who made the negative comment. On the other hand, if you are able to recognize the situation as an attempt on the other person's part to start a fight, you will be better able to ignore the comment and respond in a calm and nondefensive manner.

This part of the anger management module focuses on teaching you to identify the thoughts that make it harder for you to control your anger. You will then learn to replace these negative thoughts with coping statements that make it easier for you to stay calm and in control. This is Step 3 of the anger management process. Remember, Step 1 is recognizing your anger warning signs, and Step 2 is using relaxation strategies.

Categories of Negative Thoughts

There are many categories of negative or maladaptive thoughts. Some of the most common that you will review in group are discussed in the sections that follow.

Should Statements

The first category of negative thoughts that will be examined is *should statements*. "Should statements" are about rigid expectations of yourself and others—in other words, what people should and shouldn't do. Because people tend to see these rules as unbreakable and essential to harmonious relationships, people often get frustrated and angry when others don't abide by them. You may say to yourself or others, "He *should have* known better—there is no excuse for his behavior." The more you repeat these "should statements," the angrier you become. For this reason, "should statements" often trigger strong emotions, including those that lead to aggressive behavior.

There are three types of *should* statements:

1. *should* statements that involve a perceived violation of clearly established rules or expectations
2. *should* statements that involve a sense of entitlement—what you think you deserve or have coming to you
3. *should* statements that relate to how you think you should behave or react in a given situation

Violations of Rules and Expectations

The first type of should statement is a common one. For example, say you have a roommate who leaves his dirty clothes on your bed or uses one of your possessions without permission. Your immediate thought may be, "He knows better than that." Then you may think, "He obviously doesn't care how I feel—he just does what he wants." When you say these kinds of things to yourself, you will naturally feel agitated, because you assume that your roommate knows that he shouldn't be doing those things. It seems clear to you that someone is deliberately disregarding both the rules and your feelings.

An aggressive reaction may seem highly justifiable or even required to change the person's behavior (i.e., "Someone needs to teach him a lesson—otherwise he is just going to keep doing this kind of thing").

Identify times in the past when you became upset when someone violated set rules or your personal expectations. What did you say to yourself when this happened? Did you become angry? If so, what did you say or do to the offending party? Discuss with the group.

Sense of Entitlement

The second type of should statements involve a sense of entitlement. Entitlement means that you feel that you deserve something—regardless of your behavior. It is what you think you have coming to you. For example, you may feel that your teacher *should* drop everything he or she is doing and speak to you in your time of need, even though your teacher may be busy or talking to someone else. Or, you may feel that you parent *should* help you with your homework right away, even though he or she is busy cooking dinner. It is important that you understand that these feelings of entitlement are not rational, but they may come from a deeper place. You will need to explore this with your therapist.

Identify times when you felt entitled to something and you did not get what you wanted. What did you say to yourself when this happened? Did you become angry? If so, what did you say or do to the offending party? Discuss with the group.

How You Think You Should Behave or React

The third type of should statements involves internal pressure to stand up for yourself when insulted or challenged by others (e.g., "You should never let anyone push you around").

Identify times when you felt compelled to say or do something in response to peer or authority figure provocation. What did you end up saying or doing? Were your actions helpful or unhelpful? Discuss with the group.

Blaming Statements

The second category of maladaptive thinking that will be examined is *blaming* statements. Blaming statements are based on the belief that the deep emotional pain or unhappiness we feel is because of something someone did to us. In other words, the offending party is solely responsible for our sense of hurt and disappointment. It is important to note that this type of thinking error does not include circumstances in which a person has been clearly violated by someone else (e.g., assaulted or raped). Instead, it refers to those situations that involve being spurned or rejected in some form or fashion—for example, being turned down for a date or not getting a job. In these cases, there is an exaggerated sense of disappointment that is usually fueled by underlying embarrassment and humiliation.

There are three things missing in this type of thinking:

1. understanding that we don't always get what we want
2. recognizing one's own responsibility for accepting and dealing appropriately with such situations no matter whether we get what we want or not
3. understanding that everyone has the right to make decisions that are in his or her own best interest even if they are not the ones that we want or are best for us.

Identify times when you blamed someone else for your unhappiness. How did you feel toward this person? Did you say or do something to this person? If so, what did you end up saying or doing? Was what you did or said helpful or unhelpful? Discuss with the group.

Catastrophizing Thoughts

The third category of negative thinking that will be examined is *catastrophizing* statements. "Catastrophizing" involves greatly exaggerating the negative consequences of a situation, or, as the saying goes, "making a mountain out of a molehill." For example, you may believe that if you do not immediately react to another youth who challenges you to fight, not only will this youth have no respect for you, but everyone else will lose respect for you as well. Given this type of thinking, fighting may seem like the only way to deal with the situation. If you did not fight, you may feel inadequate and shamed.

It is important to realize that responding to every single provocation leads to a never-ending cycle of violence. Therefore, it is essential that you learn to develop more adaptive thinking in order to successfully function in society.

Identify times when you may have exaggerated the negative personal consequences of someone else's actions. How did you feel toward this person at the time? Did you say or do something to this person to get back at him or her? If so, was what you did or said helpful or unhelpful? Discuss with the group.

Replacing Negative Thoughts with Coping Statements

It is not enough to identify your thinking errors. You must also learn to replace your negative thoughts with coping statements. Coping statements are those thoughts that help you gain a sense of emotional composure and clarity on the situation. Coping statements have a calming effect and put things in proper perspective.

Take a look at your Anger Hierarchy and identify the thinking errors that make controlling your anger more difficult. Then identify coping thoughts that you can use to replace the negative ones. Here are some examples:

THINKING ERROR	COPING STATEMENT
Should statement (rules): He should know better than to use my stuff without permission; he obviously doesn't care about my feelings.	Coping statement: He has been having a rough time lately; maybe he listens to music as a way of calming down. I will tell him I don't mind him using my radio, he just needs to ask me first.
Blaming statement: I felt embarrassed when she said she didn't want to go out with me, so I have the right to get back at her.	Coping statement: I may not like it, but she has the right to go out with whomever she wants. I'm not helpless; I can ask other girls out.

Catastrophizing statement: He put me down. If I let him get away with it, no one will ever respect me again.	Coping statement: He is always trying to provoke people; no one takes him seriously anyway. I don't have to prove myself to anyone--I know who I am. No one is going to get me off-track--I have a plan and I am going to stick with it.

Homework

✎ Enter into your Anger Diary the thoughts (Column 4) that accompanied recorded episodes of frustration or anger. Identify thinking errors and begin to practice replacing them with coping statements.

✎ Identify negative or maladaptive thoughts on your Anger Hierarchy.

STEPS 4 & 5: ASSERTIVENESS AND CONFLICT RESOLUTION

Goals

- To learn about assertiveness, including the difference between assertive, aggressive, passive, and passive-aggressive behavior
- To learn the key components of assertiveness
- To develop conflict resolution skills

Assertiveness

Step 4 of the anger management process is to express yourself in an assertive, but controlled, manner. The sections that follow discuss assertive behavior, as well as other, less effective ways of expressing yourself.

Assertive Behavior

Being assertive means standing up for yourself without violating the rights of others. It has to do with expressing yourself and your wishes or needs in a firm, clear, and straight-forward manner; it does not, however, involve making threats or demeaning or attacking someone else in the course of trying to get what you want.

Aggressive Behavior

In aggressive behavior, there is some attack of the other person—either verbally, physically, or both. It is based on the belief that you can force others to do what you want them to or that violence will somehow get you what you want. When a person engages in aggressive behavior, he may end up getting what he wants in the short term, but there are almost always consequences for doing so. Sometimes these consequences may be severe and have lasting implications (e.g., suspension from school, legal charges, etc.). In the long run, aggressive behavior is not usually effective.

Passive Behavior

Passive behavior means not speaking up for yourself or simply quietly letting others take advantage of you. Passive behavior is usually based on the belief that the situation is hopeless—there is nothing that can be done, so why try? Associated with passive behavior may be a sense of fear and intimidation. People who are chronically passive may feel depressed and inadequate, and others may see them in the same way. Passive people seldom seem to get what they want.

Passive-Aggressive Behavior

Passive-aggressive behavior is a form of aggression. In other words, someone else's rights are violated or the person is disrespected through your actions. Unlike aggressive behavior, in which the anger is obvious, in passive-aggressive behavior we get back at the person with whom we are angry by not doing something that he wants or by engaging in more subtle forms of aggression, such as sarcasm. A passive-aggressive person may then proclaim innocence or unawareness that his actions have been hurtful. For example, a teenage boy may get back at his parents by getting bad grades in school or hanging out with a forbidden friend.

While passive-aggressive behavior may not generate the same consequences as aggression (e.g., going to jail for an assault), it still creates rifts in relationships and often results in retaliation. As such, it is not an effective long-term coping strategy.

Key Components of Assertive Behavior

The following are the key components of assertive behavior:

1. Use effective communication skills:
   - Maintain direct eye contact
   - Maintain an erect body posture
   - Speak clearly, audibly, and firmly
   - Don't whine or use an apologetic tone of voice
   - Make use of gestures and facial expression for emphasis
2. Express your *thoughts* as to what the problem is:
   - Formulate a nonblaming description of the problem as you see it
   - Stick to the facts (e.g., "This is the third time this week that you used my toothpaste without asking")
3. Express your *feelings* about the situation:
   - Make "*I*" statements about your emotional reaction to the problem (e.g., "I feel upset, angry," etc.)
   - Avoid blaming the other person for your feelings (i.e., don't make statements such as, "You are making me feel ...")
4. State what you *want* in specific, behavioral terms (e.g., "I want you to ask before you use any of my personal items")
5. Be willing to listen to the other person's point of view. If you don't understand his or her point of view, ask clarifying questions

(e.g., "I don't understand what you want; will you please explain it to me?")

6. Communicate to the other person that you heard his or her position.
7. Be willing to compromise when appropriate.

Conflict Resolution Skills

It is important to be able to successfully negotiate settlements to disagreements among individuals or groups of people. As you know, conflict or disagreement is inevitable in life—even best friends sometimes disagree. What is important is learning to resolve disagreements without severely damaging or destroying the relationship in the process. As with all other skills, conflict resolution has key elements or principles that must be learned and practiced.

Key Steps in Negotiating Compromises

The following are steps to take when negotiating a compromise:

1. Decide if you and the other person are having a difference of opinion. Ask the person to clarify his position on the issue. Be sure to listen carefully. Sometimes conflict arises out of a simple misunderstanding of what the other person is saying or doing. Repeat to the other person your understanding of what he is saying. Ask him if you heard and interpreted him correctly.
2. When there is apparent disagreement, explain to the other person how you see the issue. State your position clearly and calmly. Avoid making accusations or using blaming statements. Ask the other person if he understands your position. Give him a chance to ask clarifying questions.
3. When there is clear disagreement, stress that you would like to find a solution that you can both live with. Point out that you are willing to compromise, but that you want the solution to be fair to both parties. Ask the other person if he would like to propose a solution to the problem.

4. Listen carefully to any proposals that the other person may make. Do they have merit in part or whole? Where there is merit in what the other person is saying, acknowledge it. Let the other person know that you appreciate his willingness to seek a mutually agreeable solution to the problem.

5. Add your thoughts to how the conflict can be successfully resolved. While you can request changes of the other person (i.e., his position or behavior), make sure that you include discussion of ways in which you can change or compromise as well. Don't come across as being self-centered or one-sided in your proposal. Seek "win-win" solutions (i.e., those in which both parties get something they want) wherever possible.

6. When a mutually satisfactory solution can be achieved, summarize the main elements of the agreement. Make sure that both parties understand what is expected of each other. Congratulate yourselves on the accomplishment.

7. If an agreement cannot be immediately obtained, acknowledge what you do agree upon and propose that you discuss the matter again in a few days. Sometimes a cooling-off period is needed. When the problem is particularly difficult or frustrating, try to identify a neutral third party who might be able to help mediate a compromise. Be sure to end the discussion on a positive note. Comment on the progress achieved, and express optimism that a compromise can be found.

Homework

- ✎ Practice assertiveness and conflict resolution skills, if possible.
- ✎ Enter into your Anger Diary the coping skills (Column 5) that you used to manage recorded episodes of frustration or anger. Coping skills include everything you've learned in this module: relaxation techniques, cognitive restructuring, assertiveness, and conflict resolution.
- ✎ List assertiveness and conflict resolution skills on your Anger Hierarchy.

Goals

- To review the "chill out" model
- To complete the Anger Management Post-Test

Steps in Managing Your Anger—"Chill out!"

"Chill-Out" is designed to help you remember the steps of anger management:

1. Check for cues: Be aware of signs that you are getting angry. How is your body feeling? Know your anger cues (e.g., heart beating hard, jaw clenched, etc.)
2. Have a break: Relax your body. Use muscle relaxation or deep breathing. Repeat your relaxation phrase. Calm down.
3. Inspect your thoughts: What are you saying to yourself? Be aware of maladaptive thoughts (e.g., blaming statements, catastrophizing). Use coping thoughts—reframe the situation in a more positive manner.
4. Lay out your options: Think about how you can handle the situation. What are your options? Decide on the best strategy.
5. Look to be assertive, not aggressive: Express to the person how you feel and what you would like for him or her to do. Make good eye contact and speak confidently; do not use profanity or threaten the person or invade his or her body space.
6. Observe the other person: How is the other person reacting to what you are saying? Does he or she look stressed and angry? When things seem to be getting worse, realize that you may need a new strategy.
7. Understand the other person's point of view: Think about what the other person is saying. What would he or she like for you

to do? Let him or her know that you understand and respect his or her point of view.

8. Think of ways to resolve the situation: How can this situation be resolved in a mutually agreeable manner? Look for ways to compromise. Suggest your ideas for compromise and ask them for theirs.

Anger Management Post Test

At the completion of the module, your therapist will once again administer a post-test to gauge your progress and determine whether you are ready to move on to the next phase of treatment. You therapist will hand out copies of the test in group.

Anger Diary

Date	Trigger (event or situation)	Warning Signs	Thoughts	Coping Skill	Action

Anger Hierarchy

1. Low Stress (Ratings of 10–40)

Describe Situation: ______________________________

____

____

A. Trigger(s)

1. ______________________________

2. ______________________________

B. Cues

1. ______________________________

2. ______________________________

C. Maladaptive Thoughts

1. ______________________________

2. ______________________________

D. Coping Thoughts

1. ______________________________

2. ______________________________

E. Coping Strategy (e.g. relaxation technique, calming phrase)

1. ______________________________

2. ______________________________

F. Assertiveness Strategy

1. ______________________________

2. ______________________________

3. ______________________________

2. Moderate Stress Situation (Ratings of 40–70)

Describe Situation: ______________________________

____

____

G. Trigger(s)

1. ______________________________

2. ______________________________

H. Cues

1. ______________________________

2. ______________________________

I. Maladaptive Thoughts

1. ______________________________

2. ______________________________

J. Coping Thoughts

1. ______________________________

2. ______________________________

K. Coping Strategy (e.g. relaxation technique, calming phrase)

1. ______________________________

2. ______________________________

L. Assertiveness Strategy

1. ______________________________

2. ______________________________

i. ______________________________

3. High Stress Situation (Ratings above 70)

Describe Situation: ______________________________

____

____

M. Trigger(s)

1. ______________________________

2. ______________________________

N. Cues

1. ______________________________

2. ______________________________

O. Maladaptive Thoughts

1. ______________________________

2. ______________________________

P. Coping Thoughts

1. ______________________________

2. ______________________________

Q. Coping Strategy (e.g. relaxation technique, calming phrase)

1. ______________________________

2. ______________________________

R. Assertiveness Strategy

1. ______________________________

2. ______________________________

Chapter 6 *Healthy Sexuality*

Introduction

Many people, adolescents and adults alike, are misinformed about human sexuality. This module is intended to provide you with an understanding of healthy human sexuality and relationship functioning. You will learn the knowledge, values, and skills to help you prepare for engaging in reciprocal, nonabusive sexual relations with a consenting peer. This includes making decisions about when you are emotionally ready and mature enough to handle the responsibilities of sex, including the prevention of pregnancy and of the spread of sexually transmitted diseases.

Sexual urges are normal and everyone experiences them. The key is to manage them appropriately, as you learned how to do with your anger in Chapter 5. Sexual desire should become a positive life force, one that leads to greater interpersonal intimacy and joy, not one that culminates in abuse, pain, and suffering.

MALE SEXUAL ANATOMY AND PHYSIOLOGY

Goals

- To review male sexual anatomy and physiology
- To take the Healthy Sexuality Pre-Test

The focus of today's meeting is male sexual anatomy. Your therapist will start with a review of the external anatomy of men. He or she may use diagrams to illustrate.

The following sections contain basic information about the different parts of male sexual anatomy, including the penis, scrotum, testicles, and anus. Although you may feel uncomfortable discussing sexual anatomy, it is important that you learn correct information, because many young people are misinformed.

The Penis

The penis is the male external reproductive organ. Penises vary somewhat in size but the majority of them are 5–7 inches when erect. Erections are caused by the ingestion of blood into the penis. The blood flows into the penis faster than it flows out. Erections can be the result of many things—not just sexual arousal. We call some erections "spontaneous erections" because they just seem to occur for no particular reason. This often happens during adolescence. For example, a male teenager may be sitting at a lunch table in the school cafeteria and suddenly get an erection. This can sometimes cause embarrassment; however, it is perfectly normal, and spontaneous erection has happened to all males at some point in their lives.

In addition to their varying sizes, penises can also vary in appearance, depending on whether the male is circumcised. Circumcision involves the cutting and folding back of the foreskin around the tip of the penis shaft. This operation usually happens shortly after birth, but it can be done later in life. Circumcision is sometimes done for religious reasons (e.g., Jewish faith), or simply for social custom, but there is no medical reason for circumcising males. Uncircumcised males do need to pull their foreskin back when urinating or putting on a condom. Both circumcised and uncircumcised males need to keep their penises clean in order to prevent infection.

Scrotum and Testicles

The scrotum sac contains the testicles, or "balls." The testicles are where sperm are produced when a male goes through puberty.

The sperm are produced in tiny tubes in each testicle (seminiferous tubules). Millions of sperm are produced each day. Males are normally born with two testicles, with one usually hanging slightly lower than the other. The scrotum is designed to protect the testicles from injury or weather extremes. For example, the scrotum contracts (or pulls up next to the body) in response to cold temperatures (e.g., getting in a cold swimming pool). This is because the testicles cannot make sperm if the temperature is too cold or too warm. The testicles are sensitive organs and must be protected. That is why males wear athletic supporters or protective devices when playing certain sports, such as football.

Anus

The anus is the part of our body through which feces, or solid waste products are expelled. The opening to the anus is controlled by the sphincter muscles, which are located both inside and outside the anus. The sphincter muscles keep the anus closed except when feces are being eliminated.

While the anus primarily serves the purpose of eliminating feces from our body, for some people it can also serve as an erogenous zone. It other words, its stimulation can be a source of sexual sensation and pleasure. This includes both the touching of the anus and its penetration with a finger or penis. It is important to note that sexual pleasure from anal stimulation is not limited to homosexual males. It can be a source of sexual pleasure for females and heterosexual, or "straight," men, too. Because of its primary function as the means for eliminating feces from the body, however, it can be a source of harmful bacteria and transmit infections to both males and females. Therefore, males who engage in anal sex should **always** use a condom and the condom should be changed (and hands washed) before it is used for vaginal intercourse. It also needs to be noted that many males and females find anal intercourse painful or unpleasant, and not sexually enjoyable. Therefore, the sexual preferences of one's sexual partner should always be respected.

As your therapist reviews the male anatomy, please feel free to ask questions.

Healthy Sexuality Pre-Test

Your therapist will hand out copies of the Healthy Sexuality Pre-Test to you and the other members of the group. He or she will collect them and review the results with you at your next meeting. These tests will help you and your therapist set your treatment goals.

Homework

✎ Complete the Healthy Sexuality Pre-Test.

PRE-TEST RESULTS AND TREATMENT GOALS

Goal

- To go over your pre-test results and set goals for treatment

My Treatment Goals

Together with your therapist, develop your treatment goals and list them in order of importance.

My Treatment Goals—Healthy Sexuality Module

1. ______________________________
2. ______________________________
3. ______________________________
4. ______________________________
5. ______________________________

Homework

✎ Review your goals with your therapist and bring them to your next meeting.

FEMALE SEXUAL ANATOMY AND PHYSIOLOGY

Goal

- To review female sexual anatomy and physiology

Female Sexual Anatomy and Physiology

Now that you are well-informed about male sexual anatomy, you will begin learning about the female body. As he or she did at the last group meeting, about males, your therapist may use diagrams to illustrate the various parts of the female sexual anatomy.

The following sections contain basic information about the *external* female sexual anatomy (the vulva, vagina, clitoris, labia, and urethral opening), as well as the *internal* female sexual anatomy (the uterus, fallopian tubes, and ovaries). Again, it is important for you to put aside any discomfort you may feel discussing this topic so that you may learn correct information about the female body and sex organs.

The Vulva

The *vulva* encompasses all of the external female genitalia. The vulva consists of the labia, the vagina, the clitoris, and the urethral opening. The *vagina* provides an opening to the inner female sexual organs. The inner vagina connects with the womb through the cervix. During sexual intercourse, the penis is inserted in the vagina. When the female is pregnant, the baby develops in the womb and is then pushed out through the cervix and vagina at birth. The external vagina is surrounded by the *labia.* The labia are folds of skin around the vagina. The outermost fold of skin is called the *labia major* and the innermost fold of skin is called the *labia minor.* Both the labia major and the labia minor are sexually sensitive and can slightly swell when a female is sexually aroused. The swelling is caused by blood flowing into the labia. The *clitoris* is located at the top of the vagina where the labia minor converge. The clitoris is a small, pea-shaped sexual organ that is very sexually sensitive. The labia minor fold over the clitoris to form a hood. During sexual intercourse and sexual play, it is primarily through stimulation of the clitoris that a female achieves an orgasm. This stimulation can come in many forms, including gentle stroking with the finger, orally (with the tongue), and through pelvic rubbing or pressure. The *urethra* is located just below the clitoris. Urine exits the female's body through the urethra.

Internal Female Sexual Anatomy

The uterus, or womb, is the main female internal reproductive organ. The inner walls of the uterus are rich with blood vessels. The lining of the uterine walls is shed approximately every 30 days in the pubescent female. This is referred to as *menstruation,* or a female "having her period." Menstruation typically lasts three to seven days. Consistent with the shedding of the lining of the uterus, females experience some bleeding during this time. This is normal and not a cause for concern. Females use tampons or sanitary napkins to absorb the blood. Some females experience mild cramping during the menstrual process.

The uterus has two ovaries. The ovaries release eggs. Typically, one egg is released each month. The releasing of the egg is referred to as *ovulation*. When the egg is released, it travels down the *fallopian tube* to the uterus. If the egg encounters a sperm during this trip, the egg is fertilized and the female becomes pregnant. The fertilized egg attaches to the lining of the uterus, where it grows into an embryo. Unfertilized eggs are shed from the body during menstruation. Unlike male sperm, which continue to be produced throughout a man's life, each ovary has a limited number of eggs. These eggs are actually present at birth, but they have to mature before the female can become pregnant. This biological capacity for pregnancy occurs at the age of puberty and ends after the female goes through menopause. Females typically enter puberty when they are 9–13 years old. Menopause typically occurs when a woman is in her early 50s, but it varies from woman to woman. Menopause is typically a gradual process, and it culminates in the female no longer releasing eggs.

As your therapist reviews the female anatomy, please feel free to ask questions.

CHANGES DURING ADOLESCENCE

Goals

- To learn about the physical changes that occur during adolescence
- To discuss the concept of sexual orientation
- To learn about the psychological changes that occur during adolescence
- To discuss masturbation and understand that it is normal
- To learn about the cognitive changes that occur during adolescence

Changes in Our Bodies

From a biological perspective, the onset of *adolescence* is defined as entering puberty. For males, this is, first, producing sperm. For females, it is releasing fertilizable eggs. The average female enters puberty slightly earlier than the average male, although there is considerable variation in the age of onset of puberty in both sexes. Therefore, there is no "correct" age for a male or female to enter puberty—it varies from person to person and may vary according to culture or environmental conditions. Adolescence is commonly associated with the teenage years, or the years fi3–19, but it may begin at an earlier or later age.

The sexual and physical changes experienced during adolescence are triggered by *hormones*. Hormones are chemical messengers that are released by certain glands (i.e., endocrine glands) in our body. They tell the body what to do or how to develop. Certain hormones are called sexual hormones because they govern or direct change in our sexual development. Sexual hormones can be divided into two major groups: androgens and estrogens. While both males and females have both androgens and estrogens in their bodies, they are in different concentrations. Males have greater concentrations of androgens and females have greater concentrations of estrogens. The most important androgen for males is *testosterone.* Testosterone is produced in the testicles (and in smaller amounts in the ovaries). Increases in levels of testosterone during adolescence help account for the development of pubic hair in males, and hair on the face and under the arms. They also trigger a male adolescent's voice to get deeper, growth in the penis and testicles, and an increase in muscle size and strength. In females, an increase in levels of estrogens triggers the production of pubic hair and hair under the arms, the development of the breasts, the widening and rounding of the hips, and the production of eggs in the ovaries.

Sexual Orientation

Sexual orientation refers to what gender of person you are sexually attracted to. Most people are sexually attracted to members of the opposite gender (i.e., boys who are attracted to girls). This is called "heterosexuality." Some people, however, are primarily attracted to people of the same gender (i.e., boys who are attracted to other boys). This is called "homosexuality." Still others are sexually attracted to people of both genders. This is referred to as "bisexuality." There are other terms for someone who has a homosexual orientation, such as "gay," "lesbian," or "queer." "Gay" is a term that many homosexual males, and some homosexual females, use. "Lesbian" exclusively refers to homosexual females. "Queer" is a term that is also sometimes used by gays or lesbians. It can also refer to other alternative sexual orientations—such as individuals who are transsexual (i.e., changed their gender) or those who are transvestites (i.e., dress as the opposite gender). "Queer" is also sometimes used in a derogatory way by heterosexuals in referring to homosexuals. Therefore, it is a term that one should be cautious in using.

As far as scientists know, sexual orientation is something that develops very early in life. Very possibly, people are even born with their sexual orientation already established. It is not something that a person simply chooses. Often youths enter adolescence with a confused sense of their sexual orientation. Some youths may wonder if they are gay because of occasional sexual feelings towards members of their own sex. Individuals who are gay or lesbian consistently experience sexual feelings toward members of the same sex; such feelings are not fleeting or momentary—they represent how those youths typically or usually feel. You should also know that just because a person has had sexual contact with a member of the same sex, it does not make that person "gay." Sexual orientation is defined by your sexual interests or what you get aroused by—it is not simply a reflection of your sexual experiences or past behavior.

Changes in Our Emotions

The increase in levels of sex hormones in your body during adolescence, and the accompanying changes in physical appearance, can affect how you feel. Both males and females experience a heightened sense of sexuality during adolescence. This usually includes the experiencing of sexual arousal or desire. This desire may be very strong at times and create a sense of discomfort, frustration, or confusion. Changes in our bodies, and how we look, may also produce moments of awkwardness or feelings of embarrassment and sensitivity to how others view us. These changes can also make us more susceptible to experiencing depression and anxiety—especially when things do not seem to be going well or when we feel alienated from friends and family.

Masturbation

The increase in experienced sexual desire during adolescence, in both males and females, may lead to self-stimulation of the genitals, or *masturbation*. Masturbation is very common in teenage boys, and it is completely normal. The frequency of masturbation varies from youth to youth. Some youths may masturbate only once a week or less, while others masturbate several times a day. Although masturbation itself is normal, it is important for you to track your sexual thoughts during masturbatory activity. You should let your therapist know right away if you experience a persistent desire to masturbate to sexual thoughts involving children or thoughts involving trickery or force.

Another important issue to discuss is where and when it is appropriate to masturbate. Masturbation should never be done in public, in the presence of others, particularly children. It should not be done when you are supposed to be doing something else, like working or going to school. Masturbation should always take place in a private setting at an appropriate time.

Changes in How We Think

Adolescence can not only bring about changes in what you think about, but also in *how* you think. During adolescence, people develop the ability to think on an abstract level. This means that they can imagine what *might* happen or how someone *might* feel given a certain event, even if they do not directly witness it. This new way of thinking makes it easier for you to understand and distinguish right from wrong, regardless of what the rules may say.

In addition, you may be more self-centered (egocentric) in your thinking and more prone to thinking in absolute terms. Your therapist will discuss this in more detail with the group in session.

SEXUALLY TRANSMITTED DISEASES

Goals

- To learn about sexually transmitted diseases (STDs) including: HIV/AIDS, syphilis, gonorrhea, herpes, and chlamydia
- To discuss how to prevent STDs

Review of Specific STDs

In today's meeting, your therapist will present you with some basic, yet important, information about sexually transmitted diseases, or STDs.

HIV stands for Human Immunodeficiency Virus, meaning it is a virus that weakens the immune system. The immune system is the part of our body that fights off infection and disease. When it is weakened, we are more susceptible to getting sick. HIV can, but does not always, lead to the development of AIDS. AIDS stands for Acquired Immune Deficiency Syndrome. It is viewed by many medical authorities as the last stage of HIV. When people develop AIDS, they become very sick and may die. There are new drugs that can slow the progression of HIV to AIDS, and slow the progression of the illness associated with AIDS. At this point, however, we still do not have a cure for AIDS. Therefore, its prevention is critically important.

Nearly 5,000 youths are diagnosed with HIV/AIDS in the United States each year, and most of these are adolescent males. HIV/AIDS is transmitted from one person to another in three major ways: sexual contact, sharing needles/syringes, and blood transfusions (although the risk of contracting the disease this way in the United States is virtually nonexistent due to blood screenings).

The spread of HIV/AIDS through sexual contact involves the recipient's blood or skin/mucous membrane contact with the blood, semen, pre-seminal fluid, or vaginal fluid of an infected person. This can happen through oral, anal, or vaginal sex. The greatest risk is through anal sex. That is why there are proportionately more cases of HIV/AIDS in homosexual adolescent and adult males. It is important to understand, however, that heterosexual males and females can and do contract the HIV/AIDS virus. HIV/AIDS is almost always sexually transmitted through anal or vaginal intercourse.

A person infected with HIV may not know that he or she has the virus. Most people do not feel sick when they first contract the disease. It can be many years before the person experiences any symptoms. Early symptoms of HIV infection include the swelling of lymph glands in the mouth, under the arm, and in the groin. Such swellings may include headache, fever, and feeling of fatigue. If AIDS develops, the person becomes much sicker and can die. More than half a million people in the United States have died from AIDS over the past 25 years.

Syphilis

Syphilis is caused by a bacterium (called spirochete) rather than a virus. Because it is a bacterium rather than a virus, syphilis can now be cured through antibiotics. If it is identified early enough in the disease process, its serious symptoms can be averted. Before antibiotics were developed in the latter part of the 20th century, many people became very sick and even died from the disease. Initially, syphilis causes sores in the mouth, on/in the genitals, and on/in the anus. It can also cause headaches and fatigue. Over time, it can cause blindness, brain damage, damage to the heart, and damage to the central nervous system. Syphilis can be spread through different types of sexual activity, such as vaginal, anal, and oral sex. It can also be transmitted through kissing if the infected person has open sores in his or her mouth.

Gonorrhea

Gonorrhea (also called "the clap" and "the drip") is another STD that is caused by a bacterium rather than a virus. Hence, it, too can be cured by treatment with an antibiotic. Often, a males who has contracted gonorrhea experiences a painful burning when urinating and has pus drip from the tip of his penis. Many infected females, however, are asymptomatic in the early stages of the disease and don't even realize they have contracted gonorrhea. If left untreated, over time gonorrhea can cause serious health problems for both males and females. These adverse health effects include the development of arthritis and pelvic inflammatory disorder (PID). PID can cause a female to become very ill and may even cause her to become sterile,or unable to have a baby.

Hepatitis

Hepatitis is an inflammation of the liver caused by a virus. The most common type of sexually transmitted hepatitis is Hepatitis B (HBV). HBV can be transmitted through semen, vaginal fluids, and blood. Thus, it can be spread through vaginal and anal intercourse and oral sex. Its early symptoms include fatigue, loss of appetite, headache, nausea, and fever. Later on other symptoms may develop, including: jaundice (the yellowing of the skin and eyes), dark urine, and pain in the abdominal area. Although most people who contract HBV naturally get well within weeks, about 5%–10% of people never get rid of the disorder—it becomes chronic. Of those people who develop the chronic form of the disorder, about 15%–25% get very sick and die.

Herpes

Herpes is an infection that is caused by a virus. There are two types of herpes viruses that are commonly found in the human body: Type I and Type II. Herpes Simplex Type I is present in 50%–75% of adults and is very common in children, as well. It usually causes sores or ulcers to periodically break out around and in the mouth (i.e., fever blisters). These sores or ulcers may be painful, but they don't represent a serious health problem, and they usually go away on their own after a few days or weeks. Herpes Simplex Type II is present in about 25% of adults. It usually causes sores to break out on and around the genitals and anus. These, too, can be very painful and annoying, but they don't cause serious health problems for adolescents and adults, and they go away after a few days or weeks. The viruses are still in the infected person's body, however. Both Herpes Simplex Type I and Type II can result in serious health problems for newborns if they come into contact with the viruses. These problems include neurological damage, mental retardation, and even death. Therefore, special precautions are sometimes taken by physicians to lower the risk of transmission if the expectant mother is experiencing an outbreak of herpes at the time of delivery. Such precautions sometimes include having the baby delivered by Cesarean section.

Herpes can be contracted though vaginal and anal intercourse and oral sex by virtue of skin or mucous membrane contact with an open sore on the infected person or through semen, vaginal fluids, and sweat. Herpes cannot be cured, but antiviral medications may help reduce the severity and duration of experienced outbreaks.

Chlamydia

Chlamydia is another STD that is spread by certain bacteria, rather than by a virus. Therefore, it can be treated and cured through the use of antibiotics. Chlamydia usually has no symptoms, especially in infected females. Therefore, it may go undetected. Its symptoms, when present, are often like those gonorrhea and include painful urination and pus dripping from the penis. It is more common than both gonorrhea and syphilis and can cause serious health problems. Chlamydia can lead to PID in females, and it can cause both males and females to become sterile. It can also cause males and females to develop reactive arthritis, or a swelling of the joints. Chlamydia is usually spread through vaginal and anal intercourse, but it is also occasionally transmitted through oral sex.

Prevention of STDs

Besides abstinence, the best protection against contracting HIV/ AIDS and other STDs is to properly use a latex or rubber condom. This includes using condoms for both sexual intercourse (anal and vaginal) and oral sex. Condoms have the added benefit of helping protect against unwanted pregnancy. If you choose to perform oral sex on a female, you can use a shield to prevent direct contact with the female's vagina. The Centers for Disease Control (CDC) identifies several possibilities, including: a latex barrier, a dental dam, a cut-open condom that makes a square, or even plastic food wrap.

While use of a latex condom may help lower the risk of transmitting herpes, it is not a guarantee, because the area of exposure may exceed the covered penis. Therefore, it is advisable to avoid engaging in sexual activity with a person who is experiencing an episode of Herpes Simplex Type I or Type II, and for seven days thereafter. The latter is a recommended practice because it is possible for an infected person to spread the virus to another person even when they are not experiencing an active outbreak of sores. This sometimes happens because the infected person is still "shedding" the virus for several days after the sore has healed.

Sexual promiscuity also increases the risk of contracting an STD. This risk is especially high if one is engaging in unprotected sex and with multiple partners from high-risk populations, such as IV drug users and gay males.

If you are sexually active, you should be tested for STDs, including HIV, on a regular basis.

PREVENTION OF PREGNANCY

Goals

- To discuss the social, emotional, and financial consequences of teenage pregnancy
- To identify and discuss methods of contraception

Teenaged Parenting

Becoming a parent as a teenager creates many risks and potential problems for the youth as well as for the child. The following sections discuss these risks.

Health Risks

Teenaged mothers and their babies are at higher risk for various health problems. Teenaged mothers are less likely to receive proper prenatal care and maintain proper nutrition during their pregnancies. They are also more likely to smoke. They are more likely to have premature and/or low birth-weight babies. Low birth-weight babies are at higher risk for a variety of health problems, including underdeveloped organs. Death rates from pregnancy complications are higher in females under the age of 15.

Social and Emotional Risks

Being a teenaged parent means losing out on being a teenager—having freedom and doing the things that you like to do. Having a baby to take care of is a huge responsibility. It is a hard job and places tremendous pressure on the young parent(s) and their families. Most teenaged parents are unable to take care of themselves—therefore they depend on their parents for financial and emotional support. This often creates stress within the family system and takes a toll on everyone. It places both the teenaged mother and the child at a competitive disadvantage. Teenaged mothers are less likely to complete high school—approximately two-thirds drop out of school. Most are single and have to raise the child without the help of the father. Of those who do get married, about four-fifths end up getting divorced. Children of teenaged mothers are often raised in poverty. They are more likely than children born to older and married parents to fail and drop out of school. They are also more likely to be abused, use drugs, and get in trouble with the law. Both teenaged mothers and their children are at risk for developing mental health problems.

Methods of Birth Control

There are multiple options when it comes to preventing pregnancy. The important thing is to find a method(s) that you and your partner are comfortable with and use it consistently. No method can prevent pregnancy if it is not reliably used. It is important to realize that you do not need to penetrate your female partner in order for her to become pregnant. All it takes is for your sperm to come into contact with her vulva or vagina. Sperm can enter the vagina and swim to the released egg in the fallopian tube, resulting in pregnancy.

The sections that follow discuss various methods of birth control. This is not a complete list of all available means of birth control, however.

"Outer-Course"

This method refers to sexual activity that does not include vaginal penetration such as hugging, kissing, touching each other's genitals, masturbation, and oral sex. Masturbation can involve each partner stimulating themselves or each other, just so long as the ejaculated sperm does not come into contact with the female's vulva or vagina. While this method is effective in preventing pregnancy, you must be careful that the sex play does not lead to vaginal intercourse. In other words, sometimes it is hard to resist such temptation when you and your partner have become sexually aroused. It is very important to remember that prevention of pregnancy and prevention of spread of STDs are two different things. Many sexually transmitted diseases can be passed from the host to the receiver without having engaged in vaginal intercourse.

The Latex Condom

The condom is a very effective means of birth control when properly used. Data suggest that when reliably and properly used it prevents pregnancy approximately 97% of the time. Its effectiveness drops considerably (to about 85%), however, if it is not used properly or reliably. Its advantages include that it is relatively cheap and easily obtained. Its disadvantages include that some people have an allergic reaction to the latex and that it decreases sexual sensation.

The Pill

There are different forms of birth control pills that can be prescribed to females. They typically work by altering the female's hormones (estrogen and/or progestin) so that her body does not produce eggs. They are effective 92% or more of the time. Its disadvantages include that the female must remember to take the pill every day—sometimes people forget. Sometimes, there are minor side effects (e.g., weight gain or loss). Rarely, there can be serious side effects, especially for females over 35 and those who smoke. They must be prescribed by a physician and cost $20 to $35 per month. Also, the pill does not prevent the spread of STDs.

The Diaphragm, Cap, Shield

The diaphragm is a flexible round (silicone) shield that is inserted by the female into her vagina so that it blocks the entrance to the cervix. A spermicidal (sperm-killing) gel that is spread on the shield destroys any sperm that comes into contact with it. Thus, pregnancy is prevented because no sperm can enter the cervix and travel up the fallopian tube to the egg. These methods are usually effective 84%–94% of the time. Its use is associated with few health risks for the female, but its use requires examination by a physician (for fitting) and a prescription. Like the pill, it does not protect against the spread of STDs.

The Shot

There are hormonal shots (e.g., Depo-Provera) that a female can take that prevent the release of the egg from the ovary. They work much like "the pill" except they do not require the female to take a pill every day—she just gets a shot every 12 weeks. Thus, one does not have to worry about forgetting to take it. It is effective 97% or more of the time, so it works very well. It does require going to a health care professional and may cost $30 to $75 per injection. There is a temporary risk of bone thinning, and females who use it must eat a healthy diet. Like the pill and diaphragm, it does not protect against the spread of STDs.

UNDERSTANDING HEALTHY AND RESPONSIBLE SEXUAL BEHAVIOR

Goals

- To learn about healthy sexuality
- To clarify values and discuss factors that determine appropriate vs. inappropriate sexual behavior
- To critique your sexual offense(s) in light of discussed values
- To identify elements of responsible sexual behavior

Definition of Healthy Sexual Behavior

Healthy sexual behavior is not harmful to you or others, is age appropriate, and reflects good judgment or decision-making. Good judgment or decision-making includes an appreciation of societal values that govern sexual behavior.

Key Values That Guide Sexual Behavior

A value is a cherished belief or principle that provides us with guidance in making decisions about what is right and what is wrong.

Thus, values help provide clarity when it comes to making difficult decisions. We explore values when we ask ourselves, "Should I do this or should I not?"" How would I feel about it if I did it?" "How would others that I care about see me?" Usually, we share certain core values with those people whom we are closest to, including family members and friends. These values provide a basis for our relationship; they constitute common beliefs that we share with them. Such beliefs may help shape the relationships and our behavior when around those people. In the same way, organizations may promote certain values and define their mission around these values. On an even larger scale, values underpin societal customs and the laws that govern us. In this segment of treatment, we are going to explore values that govern sexual behavior and provide a foundation for sexual behavior laws. Based on an exploration of these values we can decide whether any given sexual behavior is OK or not OK.

Try to identify some factors that help determine whether given sexual behavior is considered OK or not OK in our society, then explore the value(s) that underlie the factor. The sections that follow list some key factors and their associated values. Be sure to think about why each factor (and its associated value) is important, and whether you agree with its underlying value.

Factors

Age

There are two main things to consider when it comes to age. First, you need to consider whether the sexual behavior is appropriate for someone of that age group. The guiding rule is that the behavior should be in keeping with the maturity and developmental readiness of the two people. Almost everyone agrees that sexual intercourse should be reserved for older and more mature teens or young adults.

A second important factor in determining whether given sexual behavior is OK or not OK has to do with the age difference between the two people. The rule is that the behavior should be between individuals who are approximately the same age. Given the increased strictness of sexual behavior laws in this country, it is suggested that there be no more than a two-year difference between individuals under the age of 18. The underlying value (or premise) is that the behavior should be consensual, meaning both parties want to engage in the behavior (see the next section for more information on consent).

Consent

Sexual behavior is consensual when both parties freely agree to participate. In other words, they have one another's permission and they both fully understand what they are agreeing to. This is different from forcing or tricking someone to have sex with you. Every person has the right to choose whether they want to be sexual with someone else—no one should be forced to do something that he or she doesn't want to do.

Relationship

This issue has to do with the nature of the relationship between the two people. Try to identify appropriate and inappropriate relationships within which sex can occur. Inappropriate relationships include brother and sister, parent and child, boss and employee, teacher and student, and coach and athlete. Think about the reasons why each of these is inappropriate and discuss with the group.

Appropriate relationships for sexual behavior include boyfriend and girlfriend and husband and wife. Even in these types of relationships however, sex must always be consensual.

Motivation

There are good and bad reasons for wanting to have sex with another person. Bad reasons include a desire to dominate the other person (e.g., "show them who's boss"), to "get back at" the person or someone else (e.g., have sex with another girl to get back at your girlfriend who you are angry with), or a desire to humiliate or embarrass the person. Other less desirable reasons include to have "bragging rights" with other boys or simply (and purely) for the purpose of release of sexual tension when there is little or no concern for the feelings and needs of the other person. Good reasons for being sexual include the expression of love and affection for someone you respect and care about.

When

This refers to when the sexual behavior happens. Try to identify good and bad times for one to be sexual with another person. Bad times include when a person is supposed to be carrying out some other responsibility, such as babysitting or working. It also includes times when the other person may not feel up to it because he or she is sick or emotionally upset. Bad timing may also include when you have just met someone and haven't really gotten to know each other yet. Good times are when both people fully desire to be sexual with one another and feel comfortable in making this decision.

Where

This refers to the setting or location of the sexual behavior. Sexual behavior should occur in a private setting. It should never take place in public, in front of others, particularly children.

Critiquing My Sexual Offense(s)

After you have finished reviewing the preceding sections, think about whether you agree with each rule presented and its underlying value. Think about your sexual offense(s) and list the rules/values that you violated in committing the offense(s) in the space provided.

My Sexual Offense

In committing my offense, I violated the following rules/values:

- ______________________________
- ______________________________
- ______________________________
- ______________________________
- ______________________________

Steps in Responsible and Healthy Sexual Behavior

The following steps are important for forming healthy sexual relationships:

Step 1: Waiting Until You Are Mature Enough

This is the most fundamental of the steps and should be based on a thorough review of your developmental readiness and life circumstances. You need to consider whether you are ready to be sexual with another person and can handle the responsibilities that go along with it. It is a big decision, and you should not rush into it. It is important to understand that waiting until you are "mature enough" does not only mean waiting until you're "old enough." Maturity is more than a matter of your age. It is about examining what is going on in your life at the time. Are you happy? Are you responsible? Are you functioning successfully? All of this needs to be taken into consideration before you have sex. Sex is not something you should do to escape your problems or make yourself feel better.

Step 2: Developing a Caring and Loving Relationship Prior to Sex

Sex should not be the first step in the relationship. It is important to take the time to get to know the other person and form an emotional bond with them before having sex. Ideally, sex should be the result of a loving, respectful, and stable relationship.

Step 3: Discussing with the Other Person Whether They Are Ready to Be Sexual

Remember that the decision to have sex is a mutual one (consent). Even if you feel ready, your partner might not. This is something the two of you should discuss ahead of time and not in the heat of passion. You should never pressure your partner to have sex with you, and you must always respect his or her wishes.

Step 4: Practicing "Safer Sex"

When both you and your partner have decided that you want to be sexual with one another, you should discuss which methods of birth control and protection against sexually transmitted diseases you want to use. You are *both* responsible for birth control. You should never assume the other person is going to take care of it.

Step 5: Maintaining Open Communication

Once you begin having sex, you or your partner may experience unexpected feelings. Either one of you may even start to feel that you no longer wish to continue the sexual relationship. Therefore, it is important that you and your partner maintain open communication so that sensitive issues and problems can be discussed. Even if you both want to continue the sexual relationship, it is important that you openly talk with each other about your sexual feelings and needs.

LEARNING TO RECOGNIZE AND CORRECT DISTORTED SEXUAL THINKING ERRORS

Goals

- To learn the definition of "cognitive distortion"
- To complete the Cognitive Distortions Test and discuss the results with your therapist
- To identify cognitive distortions related to your sexual offense(s)

Definition of "Cognitive Distortion"

Do you know what the word "cognitive" means? It refers to the process of thinking. A "cognition" is a thought or idea. What about the word "distortion"? Distortion refers to the process of changing or altering something so that it has a different meaning. A cognitive distortion could therefore be referred to as a "twisted thought." In the way we are going to use it, cognitive distortions will refer to thoughts that make it easier to sexually offend or act in a way that you or others would normally consider to be wrong. Specifically, cognitive distortions refer to ways in which a person minimizes the harmfulness or wrongfulness of his sexual misbehavior, or projects blame onto the victim or someone else for what he did. It can also be thought of as a way of justifying or making what he did seem "OK" or "not such a big deal."

Cognitive Distortions Test

Based on what you have learned in treatment to date, indicate whether each of the following statements about sexual behavior is true or false. Be sure to explain your reasoning in the space provided below each question.

1. Children often don't report sexual abuse because they really like it.

____

____

2. As long as you don't use force, you can't really hurt a child that you have sex with.

____

____

3. If a 25-year-old woman has sex with a 14-year-old boy, that really isn't sexual abuse.

____

____

4. Most girls secretly want a guy to be sexually aggressive and take control of the situation.

____

____

5. Most children who are sexually abused at a young age simply forget about it.

____

____

6. Even children who are not penetrated can be emotionally hurt by sexual abuse.

____

____

7. Girls who say "no" to sex really mean "yes" most of the time.

____

____

8. If you have spent a lot of money on a girl, she owes you sex.

____

____

9. A girl has a right to say "no" even if she has had sex with you before.

____

____

10. If a man is married to a woman or has been dating her for a long time, he should be able to have sex with her anytime he wants.

____

____

11. Once a girl is no longer a virgin, she should have sex with any guy that she agrees to go out with.

____

____

12. The best way for a young girl to learn about sex is by experimenting with her older brother.

____

____

13. Rape is so common these days, most girls don't really mind it that much.

____

____

14. If a boy is sexually abused by more than one male, it means that he is a "faggot."

____

____

15. If you ask a girl to have sex and she doesn't say anything, it means that it is OK to go on and have sex with her.

____

____

16. A boy can never be too young to have sex with an older female.

____

____

17. If a girl has already been sexually abused by other guys, it won't do any more harm for you to go ahead and sexually abuse her, too.

____

____

18. If you have raped or sexually abused someone, it is best to just forget about it and go on with your life.

____

____

19. Girls make a bigger deal out of rape than they should; most should just try and forget about it.

____

____

20. You can get help for a sexual behavior problem without really admitting what you did.

____

____

21. The best thing you can do after you have been convicted for raping or sexually abusing somebody is to deny it. That way the whole thing just blows over.

___

___

22. Even girls who wear short shirts and no bras have the right to say "no."

___

___

23. Guys who successfully complete sex offender treatment programs are less likely to re-offend than those who fail them.

___

___

24. It is OK to take advantage of a girl sexually if she is drunk; she should have known better.

___

___

25. If you are in a sex offender treatment program, the best thing to do is take responsibility for what you did and work hard to make necessary changes.

___

___

Searching for Cognitive Distortions

Based on what you have just learned, try to identify the cognitive distortions that made it easier for you to commit your sexual offense(s). List them below:

- ___
- ___
- ___

- ______________________________
- ______________________________

Homework

✎ Review your cognitive distortions with your therapist.

EXPLORING SEXUAL RELATIONSHIP ISSUES

Goals

- To participate in role-plays in which you discuss sexual relationship issues
- To complete the Healthy Sexuality Post-Test

Role-Plays

In this meeting, you and the other members of your group, along with your therapist, will participate in role-plays designed to help you learn to successfully deal with situations and issues that may arise in the course of a sexual relationship. Following are some potential hypothetical problems and ways of dealing with them.

Role-Play 1

You have met a girl that you like and are attracted to. She is your age and really likes you, too. You both want to have sex, but when you bring up the idea of using a condom, she says that it isn't necessary because she is taking the "pill" and doesn't have any sexually transmitted diseases. What do you say and do? You don't want to hurt her feelings, but you know you need to use protection.

Helpful Hints

Stress to the girl that using a condom is in both of your best interests—it protects not only you, but her as well. Remind her that one doesn't always know when he has a sexually transmitted disease—the symptoms may be silent for months. Point out that your use of a condom shows your concern for her and her health, and emphasize that it is a sign of respect—not rejection. If she continues to balk, then you should desist from sexual relations and begin to question having a sexual relationship with her (i.e., is this someone who has good judgment and who you can trust?)

Role-Play 2

You are attending a college that is a long way from your hometown. You try to get home at least once a month to visit your family and long-time girlfriend. Your relationship with your girlfriend is a sexual one and has been for some time. You have been thinking about her for weeks and really looking forward to having sex with her again. When you get home, you call her to find out when you can see her. Her voice sounds sad and she tells you that she just had a big argument with her mom and that she doesn't feel like going out tonight. What do you say and do?

Helpful Hints

Remember that a healthy relationship involves being sensitive to the feelings of your partner and what is happening in her life. Even though you may have been really looking forward to being sexual with your girlfriend, she may need something very different from you at this point in time. If you are sensitive to her feelings and respectful of her wishes, it is likely that she will feel even closer to you and more trusting.

Role-Play 3

You are at a friend's party and see a very attractive girl. You are 18 years old and she looks about your age. She comes over and begins to talk to you. The two of you seem to really hit it off, and pretty soon you ask her if she would like a ride home after the party. She readily agrees and tells you that she is staying with her older sister, who is a freshman at a local college. She suggests that the two of you go over to her sister's apartment and comments that her sister won't be home until much later that night. What do you say and do?

Helpful Hints

Inquire as to her age before you leave the party with her. If she is under age 18, you would be well advised to not pursue a romantic or sexual relationship with her. Even if she is 17, that could present a legal problem for you in a number of states. Inform her that you are 18 and that you can't become involved with anyone who is under the age of 18.

Role-Play 4

You have genital herpes. You have met a girl whom you really like and she feels the same way about you. She is your age and wants to be sexual with you. You are not currently experiencing an outbreak of herpes and always use a condom when you have sex. What should you do? Do you tell her about your herpes before you have sex with her, or not? If so, how would you bring this up?

Helpful Hints

Even if the risk of transmission is low, you have a moral/ethical responsibility to inform her that you have herpes. This is an important element of consent. Knowing that you have herpes, and that she could possibly contract it, is necessary to her making an informed decision. Otherwise, you are guilty of deception—she doesn't really know what she is consenting to. Bring it up in the context of wanting to be responsible and fully disclosing.

Role-Play 5

Your long-time girlfriend tells you that she wants to have your baby. You are still in school and not ready for that kind of commitment. When you tell her that, she gets angry and says that you must not love her. She reminds you that she won't wait for you forever, and that there are other boys out there who are interested in her.

Helpful Hints

Explain to your girlfriend that it is because you care for her and respect her that you don't want to have a baby before you are ready. Stress that you understand and take seriously the responsibilities of being a father and that it would unfair to her, the child, and yourself to have a baby at this point in your life. Comment that you would want to be able to give the child a good life and not have him grow up the "hard way" (i.e., without resources, an available father, etc.). Remind her that trust and mutual respect is an important part of your relationship and that you want to keep it that way. Tell her that if she can't accept your answer, then it might be in both of your best interests for the two of you to move on to other relationships.

Role-Play 6

You meet a girl at a party. She has been drinking pretty heavily all night and seems a little drunk. She is very attractive and dressed in a sexy way. She has on a short skirt and tight sweater. In talking to her it is clear that she wants to have sex with you. Both of you are 18 years old—she even showed you her driver's license to prove it. After the party she tells you that she wants to go home with you. You have a condom with you, and your roommate is gone out of town for the weekend. What do you say and do?

Helpful Hints

The fact that she has been drinking heavily all evening and appears drunk should be enough to keep you from following through in having sex with her. Even though the situation may be very tempting, she is not in a state of mind to make an informed decision—her thinking and judgment are impaired by the alcohol she has consumed. To have sex with her under these circumstances would potentially put you at risk for a charge of rape.

Healthy Sexuality Post-Test

At the completion of the module, your therapist will once again administer a post-test to gauge your progress and determine whether you are ready to move on to the next phase of treatment. You therapist will hand out copies of the test in group.

Chapter 7 *Healthy Masculinity II*

REDEFINING RELATIONSHIPS WITH FEMALES—A HISTORICAL PERSPECTIVE

Goals

- To discuss the historical oppression of women in our society
- To review goals of the modern women's movement
- To complete the Healthy Masculinity II Pre-Test

Denial of Legal Rights

Women have historically been denied basic legal rights in our country. These include rights related to voting, owning property, and transacting business. Your therapist will discuss with the group how denial of such rights have shaped male-female relationships and affected the self-esteem and psychological health of females.

In the recent past women were denied the following rights:

- Voting rights: Women did not have the right to vote in state and federal elections in our country until 1919—less than 100 years ago. This right came with the passing of the 19th Amendment by Congress in 1919.
- Property rights: In the past, married women had fewer legal rights than single women. For example, married women could not own property (separate from their husbands) until the mid-19th century (i.e., mid-1800s).
- Equal pay: Women did not have to be paid at the same rate as men, for the same work, until the passage of the Equal Pay Act of 1963. Women still, on average, earn less than men.

Goals of the Modern Feminist Movement

Feminism can be defined as the quest for equal treatment for females and the end of all forms of gender discrimination. The modern feminist movement began in the 1960s and continues today. Some of its goals include:

- general societal respect and empowerment for women
- equal rights with regard to educational, professional, and economic opportunity
- equality in relationships with males, including shared decision-making and child care responsibilities
- control over reproduction, and
- the cessation or end to sexual and physical violence toward women and their sexual objectification in the media.

Healthy Masculinity II Pre-Test

Your therapist will hand out copies of the healthy masculinity pretest to you and the other members of the group. He or she will collect them and review the results with you at your next meeting. These tests will help you and your therapist set your treatment goals.

Homework

✎ Complete the Healthy Masculinity II Pre-Test.

PRE-TEST RESULTS AND TREATMENT GOALS

Goal

- To go over your pre-test results and set goals for treatment

My Treatment Goals

Together with your therapist, use the worksheet provided to develop your treatment goals and list them in order of importance.

My Treatment Goals—Healthy Masculinity II Module

1. ______________________________
2. ______________________________
3. ______________________________
4. ______________________________
5. ______________________________

Homework

 Review your goals with your therapist and bring your completed Goal Sheet to the next meeting.

REDEFINING RELATIONSHIPS WITH FEMALES—PSYCHOLOGICAL EFFECTS OF DOMESTIC VIOLENCE

Goal

- To explore the effects of domestic violence on women

Exploration of Domestic Violence

Up to one-third of females are subjected to intimate partner violence during their lives. This includes abuse by a husband, boyfriend, or same-sex partner. The experience of this abuse has an effect on both the female and the children who witness it. Studies show that up to 84% of women in domestic abuse shelters suffer from Post Traumatic Stress Disorder (PTSD). This includes symptoms of reliving the experience (e.g., nightmares, flashbacks), avoidance of reminders of the trauma, and physiological stress. Abused women are also more likely to miss work—often because they are prevented from leaving the home or because they are embarrassed and ashamed of the cuts and bruises on their bodies. Children who are exposed to domestic violence also show signs of emotional and behavioral maladjustment. This includes an increased risk for aggression and becoming an abuser themselves. They also show more evidence of depression and low self-esteem than nonexposed youths.

Reflect on your own experiences of exposure to domestic violence and how those experiences influenced you. What did you learn from these experiences about males and masculinity? Were these positive or negative messages?

REDEFINING RELATIONSHIPS WITH FEMALES—PSYCHOLOGICAL EFFECTS OF SEXUAL ASSAULT

Goal

- To discuss the incidence and psychological consequences of sexual assault

Incidence and Consequences of Sexual Assault

Approximately 25%–33% of all females in the United States are sexually assaulted during the course of their lives. This is two to three times the rate of sexual assault of males. The risk of sexual assault for females remains high throughout the lifespan, whereas for males it diminishes when they reach adolescence. The majority of sexual assaults on females are perpetrated my males—both adult and adolescent. Specifically, males account for approximately 98% of the rapes of adolescent and adult females and 92% of the cases of child sexual molestation. Juveniles (predominantly adolescent males) account for about 15%-–20% of these sexual crimes.

Sexual assault can have psychological consequences for victimized females. The vast majority of females who are raped meet clinical criteria for post traumatic stress disorder (PTSD) in the weeks following their sexual assault. Approximately 50% continue to manifest PTSD three months after the assault, and 25% continue to show symptoms several years later. Common psychological problems in sexually assaulted women include anxiety, fear, shame, depression, and sexual dysfunction. Children who are victims of sexual assault are likewise subject to significant emotional problems. Approximately 50% of sexually abused children show evidence of PTSD following their assaults. These problems can cause dysfunction in school and in their family and peer relationships. Some of these children continue to have problems well into adulthood.

REDEFINING RELATIONSHIPS WITH FEMALES—THE EQUITY MODEL

Goals

- To discuss the concept of equal treatment for females
- To identify and discuss misogynistic messages in music and film
- To learn about the "equity" model and the "power and control" model

Treating Females as Equals

While times have changed, there is still considerable room for improvement in male-female relationships. Even today, there is pressure from society for men to be dominant in their relationships with females. Sometimes these pressures are overt, and at other times they are more subtle; you can find reference to them in our speech, our music, and in the films that we watch. At times, these messages reflect a fundamental disrespect of females and the blaming of females for the problems males face.

Negative Cultural and Media Messages

Think about the negative messages the media sends about females (e.g., in songs and movies). Discuss with the group how these messages shape the minds of young males. What is being said in these various messages about females and how they should be treated?

Equity Model vs. Power-Control Model

In years past, many males thought that the man should always be the boss in a relationship with a woman. If he wasn't, then that meant that he was weak or "henpecked" and that the woman was a tyrant. Some of these distorted ideas were based on the belief that men were stronger (emotionally and physically) than women, and better leaders. None of this is actually true, and the men who had these mistaken ideas had conflicted relationships with women. The women who entered relationships with these men were often unhappy and dissatisfied. They were not being respected and their needs were not being met. Consequently, many left. In Healthy Masculinity II, you are being taught a new way of looking at relationships with females. We call it the "equity model," because the female is seen and treated as an equal. She is your partner—not someone to be dominated. Below you will find a description of how men act and treat women within an equity model in contrast to a "power and control," or dominance, model. As you review each of these characteristics, think about how different in would be to grow up in one type of family versus the other.

- Negotiation vs. Demand: seeking mutually satisfying solutions to problems, willingness to compromise
- Respect vs. Belittlement: listening without judging, validating her opinions and feelings
- Affection vs. Coercion: show you care about her without being demanding or threatening, or touching her when she doesn't want to be touched
- Support vs. Isolation: supporting her personal and professional needs, respecting her right to her own feelings, friends, opinions

- Communication vs. Silencing: making her feel comfortable in expressing her thoughts and feelings, direct and honest communication
- Companionship vs. Oppression: respecting her reproductive rights and choices, sexual relationships based on mutual consent
- Economic Parity vs. Dependency: making financial decisions together, equal job opportunity for both
- Division of Labor vs. Dominance: sharing decisions about family matters, shared responsibility for child rearing; agreed-upon division of labor in the home

IMPROVING OUR RELATIONSHIPS WITH OTHER MALES

Goals

- To discuss traditional male-male relationships
- To learn to be open to differences
- To learn to be open to friendship with gay youths
- To learn the principles of healthy male-male relationships

Traditional "Male-Male" Relationships

Relationships among men have traditionally been about competition. Men compete with one another for various things, including jobs and women. Even in sports, men compete with one another to see who wins the game. Winning in games, as well as life, is a source of pride and reinforces your status among other men. While natural, a desire to compete can sometimes lead to aggression or violence if not properly regulated. Part of a successful society is the ability of its members to relate to and cooperate with one another in pursuit of certain goals. As in sports, it takes a team effort. And as all coaches know, truly great teams are not just a collection of talented players, but a cohesive group of players who know how to work together to achieve excellence. Sometimes coaches refer to this as "team chemistry," meaning the ability to successfully interact in a way that elevates everyone's level of play.

Males who don't learn how to successfully work with other males may become socially and emotionally isolated. Sometimes they develop strong emotional dependencies on their wives or girlfriends and expect them to always be there when they need them. This may place too great of a burden on the female and lead to problems in the relationship. This is why it's important to learn to form supportive relationships with other males. To do so, you must not be afraid to show feelings and acknowledge problems.

Think about your relationships with the males in your life and about the qualities these men had. Do you still look for these qualities in the males that you meet?

Being Open to Differences

One of the keys in developing fulfilling and balanced relationships with other males is learning to accept and appreciate diversity. In other words, another male doesn't have to look or act exactly like you in order for the two of you to become friends. Sometimes males limit themselves to relationships with guys who seem just like them. They may dress the same, use the same expressions, or even have grown up in the same area. While it seems quite sensible to look for male friends who appear to have a lot in common with you, you must remember that appearances can sometimes be deceiving. A guy who on the surface seems a lot like you may not share your most important values. On the other hand, you may find that a male who is of a different race or religion, or who is from a different part of the country, may be very much like you on the inside. Furthermore, you can grow as a person by exposing yourself to different cultures, customs, and ideas.

Being Open to Friendships with Gay Youths

One of the more difficult things for many heterosexual males is to remain open to becoming friends with males who are gay or bisexual. Some men may fear that other men and women will think they are gay if they hang out with someone who is gay. Other times there is a fear that if you become friends with a gay male, he will try and make unwanted sexual advances. It is very important that you receive correct information about homosexuality.

Being gay or lesbian is not a choice, but a sexual orientation that is established early in life—we may even be born with it. Furthermore, gays are represented in all races and cultures of the world. In the United States gays make up 2%–5% of the populations of our larger cities. They are represented in all professions—there are gay doctors, psychologists, lawyers, entertainers, and sports stars. Contrary to popular opinion, gay and lesbian youths and adults do not typically try to have sex with heterosexuals—they are more interested in establishing romantic or sexual relationships with other gays.

FAMILY RELATIONSHIPS

Goals

- To discuss family relationships
- To discuss marriage and raising children
- To complete the Healthy Masculinity Post-Test

Forming Healthy Relationships with Parents and Siblings

As many sexually abused and abusive youths know, the family home can be an unsafe and hostile environment. Unhealthy families are often characterized by a multitude of problems, including a lack of respect for one another, poor communication and boundaries, and the absence of trust and open communication. Children in such families may be subject to parental abuse and neglect, and/or exposed to domestic violence and parental substance abuse. They may also be subjected to emotional, physical, and sexual abuse by older siblings. These traumatic experiences may lead to permanent emotional scarring and result in damaged children becoming damaged adults. The abused child may ultimately grow up to become the abusive parent—a seemingly endless cycle of violence.

As we learned in Healthy Masculinity I, cycles of abuse can be broken. It is not inevitable that the perpetrator continues to abuse and hurt others. In fact, older siblings who have abused their younger brothers or sisters can help heal their wounds and prevent them from becoming angry and abusive adolescents and adults. This, of course, requires making fundamental changes in how you deal with problems and relate to others. You must grow as a person and embrace a new set of values and ideals. You must make the transformation from a negative and hurtful brother and/or son to a positive and supportive one.

Your therapist will discuss with the group the following contrasts in roles and behavior:

- Ridicule vs. Praise: Instead of teasing and belittling younger siblings, praise them for their accomplishments. This helps instill in them self-confidence and self-esteem.
- Responsibility vs. Denial and Blame: Instead of denying responsibility for your mistakes or blaming others, show your parents and siblings that you are accountable for your actions, and admit when you are wrong. This builds parental trust and shows strength of character.
- Sensitivity vs. Callousness: Instead of disregarding other family members' feelings, show a concern for them. This will demonstrate to parents and siblings that you are a caring person and not someone who is out only for himself.
- Communication vs. Acting Out: Instead of acting out your feelings, talk to your parents about your concerns. Acting out typically generates resentment, not understanding and support.
- Volunteering vs. Avoiding: Instead of shirking household responsibilities, offer to help your parents with housecleaning, lawn maintenance, and other household chores.

- Respect vs. Belligerence: Instead of angrily arguing with your parents, listen and speak to them in a respectful manner. In turn, they will be far more likely to listen to your side of the story.
- Problem-Solving vs. Complaining: It is relatively easy to sit back and complain about family problems; all that this does, however, is lower morale and make others defensive. Don't just identify problems; offer solutions that are fair and reasonable. Be willing to do your share in solving family problems.

Marriage and Family

Whether you should get married and have children is a major life decision that is best left to when you are older and more mature. Taking on these responsibilities as a teenager usually produces bad results. Teenage marriages seldom last and teenaged parents are at higher risk to neglect and abuse their children. You or some of your peers may have already fathered children, however. If so, the question for you becomes, "Can I make a positive contribution to my child's life?" In this session, your therapist will review with the group how a man can contribute to the success of his marital or intimate-partner relationship and how he can help ensure that his son or daughter develops into a happy and well-adjusted child.

Having a successful marriage obviously depends on both partners equally investing in making the relationship work. If one party has to carry the relationship, or make most of the sacrifices, he or she typically become resentful, and problems can occur. It is therefore important, before marriage, to discuss how important responsibilities will be divided. For example, will both partners work? If so, how will household responsibilities be divided? Who will pay the bills and ensure that the family stays on a budget? Do you want to have children and, if so, when? These are just a few of the many important issues to be discussed and agreed upon. To delay deciding these issues until after marriage or moving in together is to invite problems.

As previously reviewed, treating your partner as your equal offers many potential advantages to both parties. Partners who are treated as equals tend to be emotionally happier, healthier, and more invested in the relationship. They are more likely to reciprocate when it comes to doing things to make you happy and the relationship work. It is especially important to maintain open communication with your partner. This often requires making a conscious effort to regularly set aside time to talk with her about how she is feeling, her relationship needs, and her thoughts about the various problems or issues you are dealing with. You must make sure that you are likewise communicating your own feelings, concerns, and relationship needs.

Relationships need maintenance. Many times the female in the relationship will begin over time to feel that she is taken for granted and that the romance in the relationship has faded. It is important to show her that you still care for her and find her exciting and fun to be with. This not only requires verbal reassurance but the setting aside of time for the two of you to spend together in mutually enjoyable pursuits.

Being a Father

There is no more important role in life than being a father. Fathers can have a profound effect on their children's lives. This effect can be either positive or negative, depending on the quality of the parent-child relationship. In other words, depending on how you behave around and treat the child (and his mother), you can help the child grow up to be either a happy and well-adjusted person or one who is fearful, sad, and angry. It is very important, therefore, to fully understand the role of the father in families and in child development.

When the parents are present and available, children bond with both their fathers and their mothers very early in life. In fact, bonding begins shortly after birth, when mothers and fathers make eye contact with their babies, smile at them, and whisper soothing words to them when they cry. These parental behaviors set the bonding process in motion. It is a reciprocal process, meaning that there is a set of back-and-forth behaviors and emotional reactions that take place between the baby and the parent. For example, the parent smiles and the baby smiles, or the parent laughs and the baby laughs. This reciprocal process results in an emotional attachment between the child and the parent. When parents are not available, or don't emotionally respond to the baby, the baby can become sad and depressed. Babies need to be picked up and held, talked to, and played with to develop normally. It is a critical part of their physical, emotional, and cognitive development.

Sometimes new parents can be stressed and anxious when they are around their baby. If this persists the baby may become anxious and depressed, too. To feel calm and happy, the baby needs to feel loved and secure. This means that the world seems like a friendly and safe place, and he knows that there are people who love him and take care of his needs. Sometimes things get off to a good start early in life and then later, something happens or goes wrong. For example, the parents begin to argue and fight frequently, one or both parents begin to abuse alcohol or drugs, or one of the parents leaves or dies. When this happens, the child begins to see the world in a different way. It may not seem so safe anymore, and it may not feel like there is someone there who can protect him and meet his needs. He may feel worried and scared on the inside and withdraw from others. In other words, these events represent psychological trauma in the life of the child. As we have discussed, the effects of trauma can be very disruptive and cause the child to begin to have problems in school, in the home, and in the community.

This is why it is so important to not become a father before you are ready. If you do, the risk that you will not be able to properly take care of the child increases. Individuals need to be mature and stable in their own lives before they take on responsibility for someone else's life. Otherwise, their children will suffer the consequences.

Research shows that fathers are equally important in the lives of both their sons and daughters. In large part, sons develop their sense of self, and their understanding of manhood, based on their relationship with their fathers. If the father is absent or a poor role model, the son may become confused as to what it means to be a man. If he has seen his father hit his mother, or has seen his father abuse alcohol or drugs, he may think that this kind of behavior is normal. Pretty soon, and as he gets older, he may start doing the same kinds of things. In other words, he has emulated or copied the father's behavior. Sons of abusive fathers are more likely to become abusive husbands and parents. Remember, this cycle can be broken, but it takes insight, personal growth, and determination.

Fathers don't always know it, but they are equally important in the lives of their daughters. How they treat their daughter (and the daughter's mother) can have a huge impact on her self-esteem and can positively or negatively impact the types of relationships she forms with males as she gets older. Research shows that daughters who have healthy and strong relationships with their fathers are more self-confident, perform better in school, are less likely to develop an eating disorder, and are more successful in their careers. Particularly important is maintaining open communication with one's daughter and spending quality time with her. Daughters often feel that their fathers spend more time with their brothers than they do with them. When parents divorce, the daughter often feels abandoned by her father. Once again, this can affect not only the quality of the father-daughter relationship, but also impact her ability to trust other males.

Healthy Masculinity Post-Test

At the completion of the module, your therapist will once again administer a post-test to gauge your progress and determine whether you are ready to move on to the next phase of treatment. You therapist will hand out copies of the test in group.

Phase III

Chapter 8 *Empathy Enhancement*

Introduction

The Empathy Enhancement module is designed to help you develop a better understanding of the potentially harmful effects of sexual abuse. During this phase of the program, you will learn what empathy is and why it is so important, not only to you, but to your victim as well. One of the goals of this phase of treatment is to write what is called an *empathy letter*. This letter is written for the purpose of helping you understand how your victim may have felt about what you did to him or her. Please remember that the empathy letter is written for your therapy only. It is read or given to the victim only under special circumstances, and only when you are comfortable in doing so. Also, this is something you must get your therapist's approval of before doing. Writing an empathy letter can be a difficult process, but your therapist will be there to guide and support you every step of the way.

WHAT IS EMPATHY AND WHY IS IT IMPORTANT?

Goals

- To learn about cognitive and emotional empathy
- To discuss the importance of empathy in everyday life
- To discuss the role of empathy in sexual offending
- To complete the Empathy Enhancement Pre-Test

What is Empathy?

"Empathy" is being able to place yourself in someone else's shoes. In other words, understanding how the other person feels by mentally putting yourself in his or situation. It has to do with asking, "How would I feel if someone did this to me?"

There are two major types of empathy: *cognitive empathy* and *emotional empathy*.

Cognitive Empathy

Cognitive empathy refers to an intellectual understanding of the other person's point of view or needs. For example, let's say you know someone at school whose parents died in a car accident. If you had cognitive empathy, you could explain to someone else how your classmate might feel. For example, you might say that he likely feels very sad or grief-stricken. You might also guess that he would feel scared, because he might be unsure of where he would go and with whom he would live from that point forward. You might further speculate that he might feel overwhelmed and confused, and perhaps angry if the accident was someone else's fault. These are all reasonable assumptions you could make based on a general intellectual understanding of what happened and how this kind of loss would likely affect you and others. Furthermore, based on this understanding, you would know the appropriate way to act or behave around him. For example, you could express to him your condolences or sorrow for his loss. You might also offer to help him in some way or offer comforting words. This understanding would thus serve you well and help guide your behavior. It would not, however, ensure that you actually felt any of the feelings your classmate did. This is a different type of empathy called emotional empathy.

Emotional Empathy

Emotional empathy refers to experiencing the emotions or feelings of the other person. Using the previous example, you might feel sad when you think of your classmate's loss or when you see the grief on his face. While your sadness may not be as profound as his, there is still some vicarious experiencing of his pain and suffering. If you experienced these feelings you would have emotional empathy.

People can have both cognitive and emotional empathy—in fact, many people do. This is not necessarily the case, however, and emotional empathy is distinct from cognitive empathy. While both are important to successful functioning, it is emotional empathy that is likely the most powerful deterrent to abusive behavior. Imagining and then feeling the fear and hurt of the potential victim is enough to make most people stop from carrying out an abusive act. It is asking yourself, "Would I want someone to do that to me?"

The Importance of Empathy

Empathy is important in everyday life. It provides a foundation for healthy relationships. For example, it serves as a reminder of the need to treat others as we would want them to treat us. It allows for mutual respect between people and underlines the importance of fair play and not taking advantage of others. Think about the quality and nature of the following relationships and how they would be different if the people in these relationships did not have empathy for one another:

- parent-child
- husband-wife
- boyfriend-girlfriend
- employee-employer

The Role of Empathy in Sexual Offending

If you are not capable of feeling empathy, you may have less resistance to certain impulses and urges, particularly those related to inappropriate sexual behaviors. Empathy acts as an internal restraint or set of brakes on our impulses. In other words, it helps keep you from acting out in a negative way. When you have empathy, you are able to see how your negative actions can hurt others. Knowing how the other person will feel is often enough to keep you from hurting him or her. When you don't have empathy, you tend to have less guilt or remorse for your behavior. In fact, you may not care much about how your actions affect the other person.

Empathy Enhancement Pre-Test

Your therapist will hand out copies of the Empathy Enhancement Pre-Test to you and the other members of your group. He or she will collect them and review the results with you at your next meetings. These tests will help you and your therapist set your treatment goals.

Homework

✎ Complete the Empathy Enhancement Pre-Test if not done in session.

PRETEST RESULTS AND TREATMENT GOALS

Goal

- To go over your pre-test results and set goals for treatment

My Treatment Goals

Together with your therapist, use the space provided to develop your treatment goals and list them in order of importance.

My Treatment Goals – Empathy Enhancement Module

1. ______________________________
2. ______________________________
3. ______________________________
4. ______________________________
5. ______________________________

Homework

 Review your goals with your therapist and bring them to your next meeting.

UNDERSTANDING THE NEGATIVE IMPACT OF SEXUAL ABUSE

Goals

- To explore the incidence rates and effects of sexual abuse
- To review factors that influence victim reaction and recovery
- To discuss posttraumatic stress disorder

Incidence Rates and Effects of Sexual Abuse

Incidence Rates of Sexual Abuse

Approximately 10% of males and 25%–33% of females are sexually abused over the course of their lives. This is a very high rate. and it suggests that up to one of every three females is sexually abused at one or more points in her life. Discuss with the group why you think females are abused at a higher rate than males. One reason may be that boys grow up to be men who have increased ability to defend themselves against abuse as they get older. Females are vulnerable to sexual exploitation throughout their lives.

Juveniles account for approximately 15%–20% of arrests for rape and child sexual molestation in the United States each year. The majority of these juveniles are adolescent males. Teenage boys account for about 98% of the rapes and 90%–95% of the cases of child sexual molestation perpetrated by juveniles. These figures are about the same for adult sex offenders and show that males are responsible for the vast majority of sexual assaults in our society.

Effects of Sexual Abuse

Sexual abuse can result in life-long psychological and/or physical problems for the victim including the following:

1. *affective* symptoms, such as fear, depression, and anxiety
2. *behavior problems,* such as aggression, withdrawal, defiance, running away, and hyperactivity
3. inappropriate *sexual behavior,* such as the unwanted touching of other children's genitals, highly sexualized talk, excessive masturbation, and sexual promiscuity (older youths)
4. *self-destructive behavior,* such as substance abuse, risk-taking behavior (e.g., reckless driving), and suicidal gestures or attempts

Factors Influencing Victim Reaction and Recovery

Many factors may influence how a victim of sexual abuse feels and how well he or she recovers from the experience. Together with your group, you will explore the following factors:

- the victim's age
- the victim's sex
- the perpetrator's sex
- the victim's level of psychological adjustment prior to the abuse
- the relationship between the victim and the perpetrator
- where the abuse took place
- the level of force involved in the assault
- how the perpetrator gained victim compliance (i.e. other than force)
- whether the victim was penetrated
- the frequency and duration of the abuse

- how the victim's family and friends reacted to learning of the victimization
- whether the victim received counseling or treatment after the abuse took place

Post Traumatic Stress Disorder

Your therapist will spend some time talking to you in detail about post traumatic stress disorder (PTSD). PTSD is a severe reaction to trauma, and a number of sexually abused children and sexually assaulted women develop it. Adolescent boys or men who are raped can also develop it.

Major Symptoms of PTSD

The three major types of symptoms of PTSD are:

- Re-experiencing symptoms
- Avoidance symptoms
- Hyperarousal symptoms

Re-experiencing symptoms include nightmares and flashbacks. *Avoidance symptoms* include trying not to think about or talk about the event. *Hyperarousal symptoms* include being jumpy and easily startled. Think about why these kinds of symptoms might develop in response to being sexually traumatized. Why might someone have nightmares about his or her sexual victimization? What is her mind saying to her? Or, why would someone develop a fear of going out at night if she were raped in a park one evening? Can these symptoms initially serve some useful function? At what point do they become dysfunctional, or begin to cause the person harm?

Recovering From PTSD

Approximately one-fourth of people who suffer from PTSD do not spontaneously recover. Their PTSD becomes chronic and can stay with them for years or even the remainder of their lives. Common problems that persist include fear, anxiety, low self-esteem, and sexual dysfunction. Factors that may influence recovery rates include whether the victim blames him or herself for what happened, family stability/support, and whether or not the victim gets treatment. It is important that you understand how your attitude and actions can influence the victim's outcome. Positive actions on your part may make a difference in whether your victim recovers or has life-long problems as a result of the sexual abuse he or she suffered.

EXAMINING YOUR OWN TRAUMA EXPERIENCES

Goals

- To discuss the relevance of exploring trauma experiences to empathy enhancement
- To identify and discuss the effects of your own maltreatment and trauma experiences
- To explore parallels between your own trauma experiences and your sexual perpetrating behavior

Importance of Your Trauma Experiences

Nearly all of us have experienced some form of psychological trauma in our lives. Often, it occurred in our childhoods. In many cases, it involved the loss of a parent or other family member. For example, a parent, grandparent, or other person we were close to died of natural causes or was killed in an accident, or even murdered. Sometimes a parent was incarcerated or sent to prison. Other forms of trauma have to do with abuse experiences. Perhaps we were beaten or emotionally ridiculed or taunted by caretakers. Maybe we were raped or sexually abused by someone older than us. Other forms of trauma can be in the form of witnessing something that is very scary or frightening. For example, witnessing violence—seeing your mother beaten by your father or step-father or witnessing gang violence or the sexual assault of a child or older female. Each of these experiences can traumatize a child.

Learning From Your Trauma Experiences

Being abused or traumatized can lead to errors in thinking and learning, especially if there was no parent or other person there to help clear up your confusion about what happened and why.

Trauma experiences provide a basis for learning about ourselves, others, and the world about us. We may come out of such experiences an emotionally stronger person, and pre-existing bonds with supportive family and friends may be further reinforced. We may come to the conclusion that even though bad things can happen to us, there will always be certain people we can rely on, and that we possess an inner resilience that cannot be taken away from us or destroyed. On the other hand, and usually when trauma has been experienced under far less environmentally supportive circumstances, we may feel permanently damaged, helpless, and cynical about whether anyone actually cares. In a similar manner, experiencing developmental trauma may make us more or less empathic. We may emerge from a traumatic experience a more sensitive and compassionate person, or we may come out more callous and emotionally cold and distant. Try and think of some reasons why the outcome may be different for different people. In other words, why might one person come out a more sensitive person after being abused and another be more distant or emotionally closed off?

Impact on Victim Empathy

The way in which we view and handle our own trauma experiences may, in turn, influence how we see and react to other people's trauma. For example, if you were sexually abused by someone older than you when you were a child, and you blame yourself for being too weak to fend that person off, you may, in turn, blame your victim for "allowing" you to sexually abuse him or her. At the heart of this confusion may be the incorrect belief that boys should always be able to defend themselves.

Similarly, what we do with the feelings that our abuse experience(s) generates can affect our sensitivity and reactions to other people's hurt and suffering. For example, if we are largely in denial that the sexual abuse that we suffered in childhood caused us any harm, we may be likely to assume that our victim was not adversely affected either.

Exploring Your Trauma Experiences

Think about your own life and identify any abuse, maltreatment, or other forms of trauma that you may have experienced while growing up. Use the Exploring Trauma Worksheet on page 163 to identify three trauma experiences in your life and reflect on their short and long-term significance.

Homework

✎ Complete the Exploring Trauma Worksheet, if not done in session.

Exploring Trauma Worksheet

1. Purpose: Emotional trauma can result from any number of events. These include the death or imprisonment of a loved one, physical or sexual abuse, the witnessing of violence, and serious accidents wherein you were severely injured. Nearly everyone has experienced some form of trauma in their lives. Sometimes though, and as a way of protecting ourselves, we try to forget painful events or minimize their emotional significance. You may remember that avoidance or emotional blunting is one of the symptoms of PTSD. To work through and overcome the effects of trauma,we must face it. This includes remembering your feelings at the time of the trauma and examining your beliefs about what happened. Moreover, avoiding or minimizing the effects of trauma in your own life may make you more callous or insensitive to the pain and suffering that you have caused others. For all of these reasons, this segment of empathy group is designed to help you remember and examine painful events in your own life. It is believed that this will not only help you more effectively cope with the trauma, but also help prepare you to examine how your sexual offending behavior has hurt your victim(s).

2. Identify three traumatic experiences in your life. How old were you and what happened? Who did you blame for what happened?

1. ______________________________

2. ______________________________

3. ______________________________

3. Choose one of these traumatic experiences and name three feelings that you experienced at the time or shortly after the trauma.

1. ______________________________

2. ______________________________

3. ______________________________

4. Describe how you tried to cope with this experience at the time. Did it work? Did you later try to cope with it in a different way? Explain.

____

____

____

____

____

5. How supportive were others in helping you deal with the trauma? Did this make a difference in how you felt?

____

____

____

____

____

6. How did this experience change your life? For example, did it change in any way how you saw yourself or others or did it change your behavior in some way? Explain.

____

____

____

____

7. If you could go back and say something comforting to that child you were at the time of the trauma, what would you say to him?

____

____

____

____

____

EMPATHY LETTERS

Goals

- To discuss the purpose of empathy letters
- To learn the components of an empathy letter
- To write your empathy letter
- To role-play reading your empathy letter to your victim
- To complete the Empathy Enhancement Post-Test

Purpose of Empathy Letters

Writing an empathy letter to your victim is an exercise that is intended to help you gain a better appreciation of the negative impact your sexually abusive behavior had on your victim and your victim's family. It is designed to give you a greater sense of "victim empathy."

Your therapist and the members of your group will provide you with feedback on both the content and the tone of your letter. You may go through several versions or edits before the letter is ready.

Key Components of an Empathy Letter

Empathy letters contain seven major components:

1. Apology
2. Assumption of responsibility
3. Explanation of the behavior
4. Expression of an understanding of the impact of the abuse on the victim
5. Statement that you are getting help
6. Encouraging the victim to get help
7. Apology to the parents/family of the victim

It is important that you understand that the purpose of the letter is to show empathy and help your victim recover. All components of the letter should be written in a manner that is comprehensible and helpful to the victim. The letter should use language that the victim can clearly understand. Be sure to take your victim's age and level of maturity into consideration. Remember, the letter is not a chance for you to justify what you did or to get people to feel bad for you. Its sole purpose is to benefit the victim and his or her family, *not you*.

Apology

Start out your letter with a sincere apology to your victim for what you did to him or her. Think about why your victim might appreciate your apology and whether your apology could potentially play a role in the victim's recovery.

Assumption of Responsibility

Next, clearly express to the victim that you take full responsibility for the sexual offense and that what happened was not in any way the victim's fault. Remember, most victims feel that in some way they are to blame for what happened to them. Self-blame can lead to even more negative psychological consequences for the victim. This is why it is so important for you to acknowledge responsibility for your actions.

Explanation of the Behavior

This is a tricky component of the letter, and it must be crafted carefully. The intent is to help the victim understand why you did what you did, and that your actions were not the victim's fault. Your explanation should be short and appropriately worded. It should not be an excuse for your behavior and should not reflect an attempt to gain sympathy from the victim or the victim's family. It should not contain messages or language that could further frighten or emotionally traumatize the victim.

Understanding the Victim's Feelings

This is the most important part of the letter, and it should be the longest section of the letter. It is, therefore, the most difficult part of the letter to write and the section that usually requires the most rewrites. In developing this part of the letter, you need to take into consideration the age and sex of the victim, your relationship to the victim, what you said and did to the victim, how you approached and gained control over the victim, and how many times (and for what period) you sexually abused the victim. You will need to put a lot of thought into writing this part of the letter.

Explaining that You Are Getting Help

Next, explain that you are in treatment for your sexually abusive behavior and that the intent of the treatment is to lower your risk of re-offending sexually. The idea to be communicated is that you are taking steps to help ensure that you do not hurt anybody else again. It is hoped that this message provides some emotional comfort to the victim and helps reduce his or her fear that he or she (and others) will be re-victimized.

Encouraging the Victim to Get Help

This is another important component of the letter. The message to be conveyed is that it is OK to talk about what happened and that this will be helpful to the victim in the healing process. The message is, "I want you to get help for what I did to you. I have learned to talk about what I did to you, and I want you to be able to talk about it, too. Talking about feelings is a good thing, not a bad thing."

Apology to the Parents of the Victim

This component of the letter is intended to enhance awareness that in abusing the victim, you also hurt those who love and care for the victim. Thus, it promotes a fuller understanding of the overall negative impact of the abuse.

Empathy Letter

1. Apologize for what you did

2. Take responsibility for your behavior

3. Briefly explain why you abused your victim

4. Express your understanding of the impact of the abuse on the victim (i.e., how did it make your victim feel?)

5. Let your victim know that you are getting help

6. Encourage your victim to get help

____

____

____

7. Apologize to your victim's family

____

____

____

Role-Playing the Reading of the Empathy Letter

Role-playing the reading of the empathy letter in group is a critical part of the empathy enhancement module. Your therapist will guide you through the role-play and members of your group may assist and give feedback.

Empathy Enhancement Post-Test

At the completion of the module, your therapist will once again administer a post-test to gauge your progress and determine whether you are ready to move on to the next phase of treatment. You therapist will hand out copies of the test in group.

Chapter 9 *Relapse Prevention*

Introduction

In order to reduce your risk of re-engaging in sexually abusive behavior, you will need to have a plan. This plan must include an understanding of what to look out for and what to try and avoid—for example, situations and places that you should steer clear of because they put you at risk for re-offending. You also need to understand risky thoughts—those that can lead to re-offending,—and how to correct them so that you don't make bad decisions. The plan will furthermore need to outline how you will handle certain feelings that, left unchecked, could contribute to sexual acting-out—for example, what to do if you start having sexual urges for a younger child or feel like hurting someone sexually. All of this is accomplished in the Relapse Prevention module. In fact, you can think of every treatment module that you have completed up until now as a building block for relapse prevention. In each module you were taught skills, ranging from social skills and anger management skills to how to control sexual urges. In Relapse Prevention you will learn how to put all of these together so that you will have a clear plan for avoiding getting into trouble again and know exactly how and when to use the various skills that you have been taught.

The Relapse Prevention module is designed to help you:

1. gain insight into how your sexually abusive behavior came about or unfolded
2. identify factors that place you at risk for sexual re-offending
3. identify and learn to reliably use coping skills to manage those risk factors

4. draft a written plan of action (a relapse prevention plan) for how to address any problems that may arise once you are done with treatment.

OVERVIEW AND GOALS

Goals

- To learn what relapse prevention is
- To review the major goals of relapse prevention
- To complete Relapse Prevention Worksheet 1
- To complete the Relapse Prevention Pre-Test

What is Relapse Prevention?

Relapsing is falling back into an old pattern of behavior—in other words, doing something all over again. In your case, to relapse means to sexually re-offend. For someone with a substance abuse problem, it could mean beginning to drink or do drugs again. Prevention is a term you are probably more familiar with. In the case of sexual offending, prevention is about taking the necessary steps to ensure that you do not re-engage in sexually abusive behavior.

Major Goals of Relapse Prevention

As discussed in the introduction, the four major goals of relapse prevention are:

1. To develop an understanding of your sexual abuse cycle: This cycle is the chain of thoughts, feelings, and events that led to your sexual acting out. Understanding this chain is necessary to taking steps to reduce the risk that you will relapse.
2. To identify high-risk factors: These factors can be internal thoughts or feelings, or external events that increase the risk

that you will relapse and re-offend. Identifying your risk factors will help you to avoid them when they come up. If they can't be avoided, you should be able to manage them using the coping skills you've learned in this program.

3. To identify and master coping skills: As mentioned, these skills are ones that you can use to successfully manage high-risk factors when such circumstances or events cannot be avoided.

4. To integrate each of the preceding components into a comprehensive relapse prevention plan: This plan will be reviewed by your parents, probation officer, and outpatient therapist. It will serve as the foundation for aftercare planning.

Relapse Prevention Worksheet 1

Please complete the worksheet provided. It is designed to assess your understanding of the material presented thus far.

Relapse Prevention Worksheet 1

1. What does the word "relapse" mean?

____

____

____

____

____

____

____

____

2. What does the word "prevention" mean?

____

____

____

____

____

____

____

____

3. List the four major goals of relapse prevention:

1. ____
2. ____
3. ____
4. ____

Relapse Prevention Pre-Test

Your therapist will hand out copies of the Relapse Prevention Pre-Test to you and the other members of your group. He or she will collect them and review the results with you at your next meetings. These tests will help you and your therapist set your treatment goals.

Homework

✎ Complete the Relapse Prevention Pre-Test if not done in session.

✎ Complete Relapse Prevention Worksheet 1, if not done in session.

PRE-TEST RESULTS AND TREATMENT GOALS

Goal

- To go over your pre-test results and set goals for treatment

My Treatment Goals

Together with your therapist, use the worksheet provided to develop your treatment goals and list them in order of importance.

My Treatment Goals—Relapse Prevention Module

1. ____

2. ____

3. ____

4. ____

5. ____

Homework

✎ Review your goals with your therapist and bring them to your next meeting.

KEY TERMS

Goals

- To review key terms of the relapse prevention model
- To complete Relapse Prevention Worksheet 2

Key Terms

Your therapist will review with the group key terms of the relapse prevention model. Key terms are defined in the sections that follow.

Cognitive Distortions

Sometimes we misinterpret events or someone's behavior. In other words, we attach a different meaning to the behavior than what was intended by the person. This can cause us to use bad judgment or act in a way that is inappropriate for the situation. These misunderstandings can come about for many reasons. Sometimes they represent false beliefs that we acquired early in life. As we discussed in Healthy Masculinity II, many males grow up with the belief that they should be the "boss" in their relationships with females. Such beliefs often interfere with males' ability to form healthy relationships with females and cause relationship dysfunction. Other times, these beliefs are self-serving. For example, they help you justify doing something that you want to do but know is wrong or frowned upon by others. You may twist your thoughts so that you believe that your behavior isn't really as bad as it seems. Other times, you may twist your thoughts so that you blame your victim for the bad thing you did. In relapse prevention, these twisted sexual thoughts are referred to as "cognitive distortions." They are maladaptive thoughts that lead to poor decision-making. These poor decisions usually get you in trouble, so it is important to learn how to identify and correct your cognitive distortions when they are present.

Risk Factors

Risk factors are thoughts, feelings, behaviors, and events that can trigger a relapse and restart the sexual abuse cycle. There are three types of risk factors:

1. *Predisposing* risk factors: These are things that occurred in your life that increase your risk of re-engaging in sexually abusive behavior. Examples include a history of abuse, low self-esteem, and poor social skills.
2. *Precipitating* risk factors: These are risk factors that you are most likely to experience as you get close to actually offending. These include mismanaging certain feelings (e.g., sexual arousal), cognitive distortions, and deviant sexual fantasies.
3. *Perpetuating* risk factors: These are ongoing risk factors that you are likely to experience on a day-to-day- basis and include anger, lack of supervision by parents, poor peer relations, and family problems.

Cues

Cues are warning signs that you are getting into trouble or having problems. There are many different kinds of cues, including feelings, thoughts, the way other people react to you, things you say to yourself, body sensations, and your behaviors. Cues may also be risk factors. For example, feeling rejected can be a cue that you may soon begin to feel angry. Feelings of rejection can also be a risk factor separate from anger (e.g., lead to withdrawal and isolation).

Lapses

Lapses are more serious risk factors that threaten your ability to remain offense-free. Further down the chain of events that lead to sexual acting out, lapses increase the likelihood that you will re-offend. They include deviant sexual and violent fantasizing, purchasing pornography, drinking alcohol or doing drugs, and spending time alone with young children.

It is important to realize, however, that lapses do not always lead to relapse. Lapses are mistakes that you can correct by using your coping skills. If you lapse, it does not mean you are a failure and that you should give up. It just means that you need to practice the skills you learned in this program.

Giving Up

Giving up can occur either before or after you experience a lapse. Remember, a lapse is a more serious risk factor. Giving up often includes the following components:

- feeling bad about yourself
- expecting to fail
- wanting to seek immediate gratification of your needs
- thinking/judgment errors

Coping Responses

Coping responses are strategies that you can use to maintain your self-control and prevent yourself from relapsing. Some helpful strategies include relaxation and assertiveness skills. At times, you may feel the best way to cope in the face of a high-risk situation is to do something you used to do in the past; maybe something like drinking or using drugs. These are not helpful coping strategies. These types of coping only make it more likely that you will relapse and sexually re-offend. It is important to remember to use the skills you learned in treatment, not the maladaptive skills you relied on in the past.

Relapse Prevention Worksheet 2

Please complete the worksheet provided. It is designed to assess your understanding of the material presented thus far.

Relapse Prevention Worksheet 2

Mark each statement "true" or "false."

1. A risk factor is anything that increases your chance of sexually re-offending. It can be a thought, feeling, or event. **True False**

2. Even though putting yourself in a high-risk situation (e.g., babysitting) may increase the odds that you will sexually act- out, it is better to face these situations than avoid them. Otherwise, you will never develop confidence in you ability to handle difficult situations. **True False**

3. A cognitive distortion cannot be a risk factor. **True False**

4. A "predisposing" risk factor is something that you experience as you get close to sexually re-offending.—for example, having a sexual fantasy about a child. **True False**

5. A "perpetuating" risk factor is something that has been in your life for a long time that increases your risk of sexually re-offending. For example, you have always had poor self-esteem and felt more comfortable around younger children than people your own age. **True False**

6. A "precipitating" risk factor is something that keeps you at risk for sexually re-offending. For example, you associate with a delinquent peer group and they think it is funny when you touch girls whom you don't know on the butt. **True False**

7. A "cue" is a warning sign that you may be getting yourself in trouble. **True False**

8. Feelings of rejection can be both a cue and a risk factor. **True False**

9. A "lapse" occurs early in the sexual abuse cycle. It is like a cue in that it warns you that you may be getting into trouble. **True False**

10. Once you have lapsed, it is pretty much impossible to stop yourself from sexually re-offending. You may as well give-up. **True False**

11. Giving up can occur before or after you experience a lapse. It may include feeling bad about yourself and expecting to fail. It makes it easier to give-in to the sexual impulse. **True False**

12. "Coping responses" are positive things you can do to maintain control over your sexual behavior. For example, when you have a sexual urge you can practice "Stop and Think." **True False**

13. A "trigger" is something that sets the sexual abuse cycle in motion. For example, seeing a young child alone on a playground may trigger sexual thoughts. **True False**

14. Sexual offending may trigger feelings of guilt and shame. To get rid of these feelings, the offender may try and blame the victim or someone else for what happened. This is called "justification." **True** **False**

15. As you attempt to justify your sexual offending behavior, you may begin to feel sorry for yourself and engage in a downward spiral of self-pity. This might actually re-trigger another cycle of sexual acting out. **True** **False**

Homework

✎ Complete Relapse Prevention Worksheet 2, if not done in session.

UNDERSTANDING THE SEXUAL ABUSE CYCLE

Goals

- To learn about the sexual abuse cycle
- To review key terms
- To discuss phases in the sexual abuse cycle
- To practice constructing your own sexual abuse cycle
- To complete the first section of Relapse Prevention Worksheet 3

The Sexual Abuse Cycle

Your sexually abusive behavior represents a chain of thoughts, feelings, behaviors, and events that unfolded over time. In other words, before you actually engaged in the sexually abusive behavior, you entertained certain thoughts and had certain feelings. These feelings and thoughts were connected and led to a series of actions. You did not simply see the victim and immediately run over and commit a sexual offense. There were several, and often many, intervening steps. Understanding how one thing led to another, until the sexual abuse occurred, is a major goal of relapse prevention. This is called "understanding your sexual abuse cycle."

Understanding your cycle is necessary for the simple reason that it is very difficult to prevent something from happening that you don't understand or see coming. Once you understand the links among a series of thoughts, feelings, and behaviors, you can take steps to prevent this chain reaction from reoccurring. On the other hand, if you don't do this, you may inadvertently do the same thing all over again. That is where the word "cycle" comes in. In a cycle, things repeat themselves. Over time, cycles become habits, or things that you naturally do. Sexual abuse can become cyclic or habitual over time. Such cycles may become stronger and more ingrained with repetition, and thus harder and harder to break.

Cycle Components

Your therapist will review with the group the components of the sexual abuse cycle. Components are described in the sections that follow.

Triggers

The sexual abuse cycle starts with a "trigger." Triggers are events that start the chain or set the cycle in motion. A trigger could be watching a pornographic movie or looking at a pornographic magazine. A triggering event is not always sexual in nature, however. It can be something like getting a bad grade in school, being rejected by a girl, or being asked to babysit.

Thoughts

Thoughts follow the triggering event. After the triggering event, a thought comes to mind. For example, pornography may trigger the thought in someone that he would like to try the sexual behavior shown in the movie or magazine. This person might wonder what it would be like to do those things with a girl. Getting a bad grade or being rejected by a girl might produce thoughts that he is a "loser" and can't compete with other boys. Being asked to babysit might produce the thought that his parents are always infringing on his spare time.

Feelings

The triggering event and subsequent thought(s) may in turn produce certain feelings or emotions. In the example of the youth who was viewing pornography, thinking about how he would like to try the things he saw might produce feelings of sexual excitement. Thoughts of being a "loser" might evoke feelings of sadness, and thoughts of his parents infringing on his spare time might produce feelings of resentment or anger.

Behaviors

Actions often follow feelings. The feeling of sexual arousal might lead to masturbatory behavior. Feelings of sadness might lead to social withdrawal, and feelings of resentment and anger might lead to sarcastic comments or oppositional behavior.

Events/Actions of Others

Often, certain events occur in the middle of the cycle that can affect your thinking, feelings, and behavior. These include the actions of others, including the victim's response to your actions and comments.

Phases of Sexual Abuse Cycle Phases

As a sexual abuse cycle becomes habitual, it often has distinct phases. These are discussed in the sections that follow.

"Pretends-To-Be-Normal" Phase

In the sexual abuse cycle, there are various problem areas that serve as early warning signals that you are at risk of re-enacting the cycle and relapsing. These warning signs indicate that there is something wrong with how you are thinking, feeling, and/or acting in response to life problems and situations. Often, even when these warning signs occur, you may not acknowledge that trouble is looming. You may pretend that everything is normal. In order to prevent re-enacting the cycle, you must identify the problem area (or areas) being experienced and take positive steps to lower the risk of re-offending. The following are common problem areas and warning signs you may experience. Problems in one or more of these areas can serve as triggers to the "build-up" phase and sexual acting out.

- Self-esteem
- Anger
- Family
- Peers/friends/social life
- School
- Employment
- Financial
- Drugs and alcohol
- Leisure time activities
- Marital/dating
- Health and physical appearance

"Build-Up" Phase

If you don't address problems because you are pretending that everything is normal, you run the risk of entering the "build-up" phase of the sexual abuse cycle. The build-up phase consists of chains of thoughts, feelings, and behaviors that are risk factors for sexual acting out. When you enter the build-up phase, it is important that you understand your risk factors and intervene as soon as you recognize the potential for lapsing. If you do not interrupt the build-up phase, a lapse is likely to occur.

"Acting-Out" Phase

The "acting out" phase is just that; the phase of the sexual abuse cycle in which you engage in sexually abusive behavior. Acting out can serve several functions, such as getting rid of pent-up emotions like anger and resentment; gaining control and a sense of power; and relieving tension and getting sexual gratification. While acting out may make you feel better in the short run, it leads to major life problems and has potentially serious consequences (e.g., getting arrested, alienating family and friends). Therefore, the overall goal of relapse prevention is to learn to use positive coping strategies and prevent acting out (i.e., sexually re-offending).

"Justification" Phase

You may experience shame, guilt, fear, and despair after acting out sexually. To get rid of these feelings, you may try to minimize what you did or blame the victim (or others). As you attempt to justify your behavior, you may begin to feel sorry for yourself and engage in a downward spiral of self-pity and self-absorption. Often, when a person enters this phase, he may make short-lived promises to not offend again or attempt to convince himself that his problem will simply go away with time. These erroneous thoughts may only lead to re-entering the "pretends to be normal" phase, starting the sexual abuse cycle all over again.

Relapse Prevention Worksheet 3

Use the following example and the first section of Relapse Prevention Worksheet 3 at the end of the chapter to guide you in creating your own sexual abuse cycle.

- *Trigger* (overheard friends talking about their sexual exploits) ⟶
- *Thought* (everybody but me is having sex) ⟶
- *Feeling* (embarrassment) ⟶
- *Behavior* (walk away from everybody and leave the room) ⟶
- *Thought* (I wonder what it would be like to have sex) ⟶
- *Feeling* (frustration) ⟶
- *Behavior* (go home) ⟶

- *Thought* (I'll go check out some porn) ⟶
- *Feeling* (nervous excitement) ⟶
- *Behavior* (go to bedroom and log on to a porn Web site) ⟶
- *Thought* (I really want to have sex with a girl) ⟶
- *Feeling(s)* (frustration and arousal) ⟶
- *Event/Behavior* (little sister knocks on my door/I ask who it is) ⟶
- *Thought* (maybe I can trick her into performing oral sex on me) ⟶
- *Feeling* (scared but excited) ⟶
- *Behavior* (let her in and lock the door) ⟶
- *Thought* (if she sees a picture of it maybe she will want to try it) ⟶
- *Feeling* (more excited but still nervous) ⟶
- *Behavior* (have her sit on my lap while I show her pornography) ⟶
- *Thought* (I'll tell her we are going to make our own movie) ⟶
- *Event* (she laughs and asks me what the people in the pictures are doing) ⟶
- *Feeling* (more relaxed/very sexually excited)⟶
- *Behavior* (start to unzip pants)

Homework

✎ Complete the first section of Relapse Prevention Worksheet 3 on page 192, if not done in session.

Goals

- To review the different types of high risk factors
- To identify your own high risk factors and their roles in your sexual abuse cycle

Types of High Risk Factors

A high risk factor is something that increases the chance that you will sexually act out in an abusive or exploitive manner. Risk factors can be 1) external situations, 2) certain behaviors you engage in, 3) emotions/feelings, and 4) thoughts. Risk factors should be avoided whenever possible. Avoidance is the smartest and most effective risk-management strategy. It keeps you away from potentially dangerous situations. When risk factors cannot be avoided, you must be extra careful and prepared to use coping strategies for staying in control.

Risky Situations

Depending on the offense you committed, different *external situations* can act as high-risk factors. If your offense involved a child, external situations would include places like playgrounds, video arcades, schoolyards, and other places where children congregate. Another external situation would be one in which you are alone with a younger child, like babysitting or tutoring. If these situations are high risk factors for you, it is absolutely necessary for you to avoid being alone with younger children.

If you committed your offense under the influence of drugs or alcohol, risky situations may include parties at which other people are using substances or at which there is easy access to substances. Watching your friends drink or get high may create a strong desire to join in the fun. A risky situation may also include being alone at home, if your parents keep alcohol in the house that you can easily get your hands on.

If you committed your offense in the presence of negative peers, risky situations may include going to the homes of these "friends" or going to public places where these people hang out.

Risky Behaviors

Risky behaviors are those that increase the risk that you will ultimately engage in sexually abusive behavior. Such behavior may trigger urges to sexually act out, or it may lower inhibitions to the same. An example would be horseplay with children. The physical contact in horseplay may prove sexually stimulating and lead to sexual thoughts and/or overt sexual behavior. Viewing pornography represents risky behavior for many youths. It creates strong sexual arousal and may depict sexual behavior that they would like to experiment in.

Risky Feelings and Emotions

Any number of emotions or feeling states may contribute to the risk of sexually acting out. Anger commonly plays such a role. Anger can contribute to sexual acting out in a number of ways. For example, when some people get angry, they adopt an "I don't care attitude." When this happens, they may give themselves permission to give in to a sexual urge that they know will get them into trouble. Anger may also fuel cognitive distortions. If we are angry with someone, we may make excuses for engaging in abusive behavior. Sometimes people blame others for their actions and feel justified in their abusive behavior. For example, a person who sexually abused a girl may justify his actions by saying something like, "She was teasing me, so she got what she was asking for." Other emotional states that can give rise to sexually abusive behavior include jealousy and depression.

Risky Thoughts

Certain thoughts can be risky, as well. For example, sexually fantasizing about a child or the engagement in sexually inappropriate behavior (e.g., public masturbation) may lead to heightened arousal and the desire to engage in the behavior. Cognitive distortions represent risky thoughts because they contribute to minimizing the seriousness of the misbehavior, its consequences for the victim or perpetrator, or the perpetrator's responsibility for the act.

Identifying Risk Factors

In the second section of Relapse Prevention Worksheet 3, list your specific risk factors. You should be able to explain how each listed factor increases your chance of engaging in sexually abusive behavior and where each factor might occur in your sexual abuse cycle (see the first section of Worksheet 3). For example, is the listed risk factor a "trigger," a "thought," a "feeling," or a "behavior" and when does it occur in the sexual abuse cycle?

Homework

✎ Complete the second section of Relapse Prevention Worksheet 3 on page 192, if not done in session.

IDENTIFYING COPING SKILLS

Goals

- To review the coping skills you have learned in this program
- To discuss when and how specific coping skills will be used in your relapse prevention plan

Review of Coping Skills

You have acquired a number of useful coping skills since beginning treatment. These include social skills, impulse-control skills, and anger-management skills. You have also acquired pro-social values (e.g., respect for self and others) and developed a greater capacity to empathize with others. Each of these skills can be used in the relapse prevention process.

For example, the "Stop and Think" procedure (see Chapter 5) lends itself to curbing sexual urges to act out. If you are tempted to accept a babysitting invitation, you can "switch" to the imagined consequence of re-offending and having to face new legal charges. You can also use the "escape" portion of this procedure to imagine the positive things that will come your way if you practice good impulse control and judgment.

When feeling lonely, you can use you social skills to seek out new friends. These include introducing yourself and getting to know a new student at school, or asking a friend to do something after school. Social skills can also be used in a number of additional ways, such as talking to your parents about what you are going through or asking them for help in dealing with things that you are worried about.

Several anger- and stress-management skills were taught and can be used to help prevent you from re-enacting the sexual abuse cycle. These include calming strategies such as progressive muscle relaxation and cue-controlled breathing. They also include examining your cognitions to avoid "should statements" and "catastrophizing," and replacing these types of thoughts with more helpful ones. You also learned some very useful anger management skills such as assertiveness and conflict resolution.

You should not limit yourself to the skills you learned in previous phases of treatment. There are many other coping skills that you can and should learn to use. These include avoiding or removing yourself from high-risk situations, calling a friend, parent, or therapist for help when you feel desperate or tempted to do something wrong, and writing down your feelings in a diary. Exercising and playing sports are other ways of getting your mind off sexual urges and getting rid of pent up emotions.

Identifying Coping Skills for Relapse Prevention

Return to your partially completed Relapse Prevention Worksheet 3 and list the coping skills you will use to prevent relapsing in the final section of the worksheet. Make sure to identify specific coping skills for each risk factor you identified and explain when and how you will use these skills. It is important that you have more than one coping skill available for each situation or problem that may develop.

Homework

✎ Complete the final section of Relapse Prevention Worksheet 3 on page 192, if not done in session.

YOUR RELAPSE PREVENTION PLAN

Goals

- To develop a written relapse prevention plan
- To present your relapse prevention plan to those involved (therapist, parents, probation officer, etc.)
- To complete the Relapse Prevention Post-Test

Developing Your Written Relapse Prevention Plan

So far, you have constructed your sexual abuse cycle, identified your risk factors, and reviewed the coping skills you have learned in treatment. Now, you will use all of this information to create your individual relapse prevention plan. Refer back to your partially completed Relapse Prevention Worksheet 3. This is what forms the base of your relapse prevention plan.

Please review the worksheet with your therapist and complete Section IV. Your therapist will keep a copy of this plan for his or her records. You will keep the original and share it with your parents or guardians.

Presenting Your Relapse Prevention Plan

You will present your relapse prevention plan in group as practice for presenting the plan to your family or guardian. Where appropriate, you may present your relapse prevention plan to your probation officer and judge. Each may have suggestions for further strengthening your plan. Once you have presented your relapse prevention plan and incorporated helpful feedback, you should go over it with your therapist and get his or her final approval. Your finalized relapse prevention plan should be signed by your therapist and your parent or guardian. It is recommended that you keep a copy in a safe place in your home and give a copy to your parent or guardian. If you are involved with the court or social services, you may also want to give a copy to your caseworker. You should frequently review your relapse prevention plan and remain aware of its various components. It is recommended that you do this at least once a week for the first six months after you have completed the program. You should review it at least monthly thereafter. Please remember that as events occur and things change in your life, your relapse prevention plan may need revision. This is best done under the guidance of a therapist who is familiar with you and has experience treating youths with sexual behavior problems. It should also be done with the support and involvement of your parent/guardian.

Relapse Prevention Post-Test

At the completion of the module, your therapist will once again administer a post-test to gauge your progress and determine whether or not you are ready to move on to the next phase of treatment. You therapist will hand out copies of the test in group.

Homework

✎ Complete your written relapse prevention plan by signing Section IV of Relapse Prevention Plan Worksheet 3.

Relapse Prevention Worksheet 3

I. Identify the key steps in your sexual assault cycle

Trigger (Event)(____________________) ⇨ *Thought* (____________________) ⇨

Feeling (____________________) ⇨ *Behavior* (____________________) ⇨

Thought (____________________) ⇨ *Feeling* (____________________) ⇨

Behavior (____________________) ⇨ Thought (____________________) ⇨

Feeling (____________________) ⇨ Behavior (____________________) ⇨

Thought (____________________) ⇨ Feeling (____________________) ⇨

Behavior (____________________) ⇨ Thought (____________________) ⇨

Feeling (____________________) ⇨ Behavior/Offense (____________________) ⇨

Identify Cues: ____

Identify the Lapse: ____

II. Identify Risk Factors

A. External

1. ____
2. ____
3. ____

B. Internal

1. ____
2. ____
3. ____

III. Identify potentially effective coping strategies and indicate when (at what point) you would use them to stop the cycle from being re-enacted.

1. ____
2. ____
3. ____
4. ____
5. ____

IV. Pledge

I understand the steps in my sexual assault cycle and my high risk factors. I also have learned coping skills to lower my risk of re-offending. I pledge to do my very best to avoid high-risk situations and use the learned coping skills to prevent my ever re-engaging in sexually abusive behavior. In support of this commitment, I promise to maintain open communication with my parent/guardian and review the contents of my relapse prevention plan on a regular basis.

Signature of Client Date:

___

Signature of Parent/Guardian Date:

___

Signature of Referral Agent Date:

___

Chapter 10 *Healthy Masculinity III*

Introduction

Your treatment is aimed at helping you learn to live a healthy and productive life. Living a healthy and productive life goes beyond simply not engaging in sexually abusive behavior. It means having a well-rounded life and achieving happiness and success in all of the things you choose to do. This includes your relationships with family and friends, your education and career, and your physical and mental health. To achieve these things, you will need to have a life plan. A life plan is needed because good things in life seldom happen by chance alone. Instead, they generally happen because we have made good decisions and worked hard to achieve success. Healthy Masculinity III is designed to help you start developing a life plan. This will include creating a "vision" for your life and coming up with positive, attainable goals for your education, career, and family.

Your life plan should be grounded in reality and include a vision of who and what you want to become. It must be holistic and include short, intermediate, and long-term goals in all major areas of your life. Furthermore, it must be accompanied by a clear plan of action. It is okay, however, to be flexible with your goals and dreams. Sometimes plans change, and you have to pursue an alternative path. What is important is that you have a sense of direction. In other words, you know the kind of life you want to live and what you eventually want to achieve as a person.

Goals

- To learn the focus of Healthy Masculinity III
- To talk about the importance of dreams and goals
- To complete the Healthy Masculinity III Pre-Test

Focus of Healthy Masculinity III

As described in the introduction, this module of the curriculum is designed to help you establish a vision for how you would like to live your life and develop attainable life goals in support of this vision. While your vision and the accompanying goals should be inspirational, they need to be attainable and grounded in reality. Don't be intimidated by this task. You may not know at this point what you want to do with the rest of your life, and that's OK. You can always change your mind at some point in the future about the particulars of what you want to do or accomplish.

Importance of Dreams and Goals

It is important to have "dreams." Dreams can energize us and give us a sense of direction. In fact, they can inspire us to achieve greatness.

Having dreams involves forming a vision or picture of what you want to become or see happen in your life. Dreams typically reflect your values and ideals—what you think is important and admirable. For example, some people may have big dreams of curing a disease, while others may have more personal dreams, such as creating a better life for their families. Regardless of whether your dreams are large or small, you must create and follow a plan to achieve them. Otherwise, dreams remain simply that—things that you imagine but never see through to fruition.

Every person needs a road map for how to make his dream a reality. This involves thinking about all of the necessary steps that it will take to get to where you want to go. It also involves setting short-term, intermediate, and long-term goals. For example, if your long-term goal is to become a physician, lawyer, or psychologist, then an intermediate goal may be making the Honor Roll this semester. A short-term goal may be making a "B" or higher on an upcoming English test.

Use the worksheet provided to map out the steps you need to take in order to achieve your dreams. Be sure to list your dream at the top and then list all the short-term, intermediate, and long-term goals you will need to accomplish before you can make your dream a reality.

My Dream

Short-term goals

1.
2.
3.
4.
5.

Intermediate Goals

1.
2.
3.
4.
5.

Long-term Goals

1.
2.
3.
4.
5.

Healthy Masculinity III Pre-Test

Your therapist will hand out copies of the Healthy Masculinity Pre-Test to you and the other members of the group. He or she will collect them and review the results with you at your next meeting. These tests will help you and your therapist set your treatment goals.

Homework

✎ Complete the Healthy Masculinity III Pre-Test.

PRE-TEST RESULTS AND TREATMENT GOALS

Goal

- To go over your pre-test results and set goals for treatment

My Treatment Goals

Together with your therapist, use the worksheet provided to develop your treatment goals and list them in order of importance.

My Treatment Goals—Healthy Masculinity III Module

1. ______________________________
2. ______________________________
3. ______________________________
4. ______________________________
5. ______________________________

Homework

✎ Review your goals with your therapist and bring them to your next meeting.

Goals

- To discuss the concept of the "generative male"
- To work toward adopting the generative male ideal in your own life

The "Generative Male"

The "generative male" is a man who achieves his sense of self-worth and self-esteem through his demonstrated respect for self and others, his ability to give, and his commitment to his family, his community, and the larger society in which he lives. The generative male is, therefore, one who rises above his own selfish interests and thinks about the needs and rights of others. Generative males are dedicated to helping other people and making their communities, and the world at large, a better place to live.

Adoption of the Generative Male Ideal

Think about how you have lived your life thus far and whether you have followed the generative male ideal. If you haven't, what changes do you need to make? Use the space provided to list some of the things you need to do in order to achieve the generative male ideal. What personal sacrifices will you have to make? Are you ready to make them?

____

____

____

Homework

✎ Record your thoughts about becoming a "generative male" in the space provided in the workbook, if not done in session.

DEVELOPING A LIFE VISION

Goals

- To discuss the meaning of having a life vision
- To define your life vision

What is a Life Vision?

Having a life vision involves deciding what is most important to you. This includes deciding how you want to live your life and what kind of person you want to be known as. The formation of a life vision is closely tied to your personal values.

In group, you will explore the values that you hold dear that influence your thinking about what you want to do with your life. Return to the theme of the generative male. Do your own values parallel those implied in the definition of the generative male? Discuss with the group.

Defining Your Life Vision

Together with your therapist, you will develop a vision for your life. Start by listing the values that are most important to you, and then use these values to define the kind of person you would like to become—your ideal self. Once you have defined your ideal self, elaborate on the kind of relationships you would like to have with family and friends, and what kind of acts or deeds you would like to perform. Use the worksheet provided to complete this exercise.

Homework

- ✎ Use the worksheet provided to write a short essay titled, "My Life's Vision."
- ✎ Be sure to bring your completed essay to the next meeting.

Goal

- To explore the importance of education

The Importance of Education

As you probably know, getting a good education is vitally important in today's world. Education affords you lifestyle and economic advantages. There are more job opportunities for people who finish high school than for those who do not. Also, there are more job opportunities for those who finish high school and continue on to either a higher level of education (college) or to vocational training. Higher education and vocational training leads to more and better (i.e., more rewarding) job choices.

Homework

✎ Use the worksheet provided to write a short essay that describes your educational goals. What level of education/vocational training do you aspire to and how do you envision this happening? For example, do you plan on getting additional vocational training or attending college after high school, or do you plan to first take some time off from your studies?

✎ Be sure to bring your completed essay to the next meeting.

My Educational Goals

Goal

- To learn about different career options

Career Options

There are many different types of work that people do. Here are some general categories of work that you may be interested in:

- Healthcare: doctor, nurse, physical therapist, dietician, personal trainer, etc.
- Education: teacher, coach, school principal, guidance counselor, etc.
- Banking and finance: bank teller, loan officer, stock broker, accountant, etc.
- Building and construction: architect, draftsman, carpenter, mason, plumber, etc.
- Hospitality: waiter, chef, restaurant manager, host, etc.

Think about what type of career you are interested in, and begin thinking about the steps you need to get a job in your chosen field. Use the following list to guide you as you research career options:

1. How much training does the job require?
2. Where do I get the education/training necessary?
3. What is the average salary for this job?

Homework

✎ Use the worksheet provided to write a short essay about your career goals and interests.

✎ Be sure to bring your completed essay to the next meeting.

My Career Goals

Goals

- To discuss family relationship goals
- To discuss other relationship goals

Family Relationship Goals

In group, you will be asked to reflect on your family relationship goals. Think about the types of relationships you want to have with your family members. How can you establish healthy relationships with those close to you? How can you repair relationships that may have been damaged? Which relationships do you want to continue to invest in and which may be beyond repair?

Think also about how you envision the family you may want to start in the future. Do you think that you might want to get married some day or have children? If so, what kind of husband and/or father do you want to be? If you want to get married and have children, do you want to be like or different from your own father? If so, how and why?

Other Relationship Goals

Similarly, think about the kind of relationships you would like to have with others, such as friends, neighbors, and co-workers. For example, what kind of friend do you want to be, and why is this important to you? Have you been this type of friend in the past? If not, what got in the way of that happening?

Homework

✎ Use the worksheet provided to write a short essay about your relationship goals.

✎ Be sure to bring your completed essay to the next meeting.

My Relationship Goals

Goals

- To discuss the importance of good hygiene and appearance
- To discuss the benefits of maintaining good health

Importance of Hygiene and Appearance

During adolescence, your body goes through many changes. For example, you will grow body hair (on your face, on your chest, etc.) making it necessary to shave. Puberty also affects your glands, so it is important to bathe regularly and use deodorant. Keeping up with your hygiene and appearance is important because it shows others that you care about yourself and that you want to make a good impression. People are more attracted to others who are well put together. Being neatly groomed makes you more approachable. It can help you attract friends, romantic partners, and can even help you get and keep a job.

Benefits of Good Health

Good health gives you an enhanced sense of well-being and vitality, greater energy and stamina, and improved physical appearance. Poor health, on the other hand, can do just the opposite. It can drain you of energy and worsen your appearance. Poor health also has financial implications—for example, it can lead to an increased cost due to extra doctor's visits, medications, and hospitalizations. Many diseases, such as diabetes and heart disease are brought on by poor health habits, such as obesity, smoking, and alcohol abuse. You can prevent illness and the risk of developing a chronic disease by avoiding risky behavior (e.g., smoking) and engaging in regular exercise, eating a healthy diet, and getting adequate rest.

Goals

- To discuss the importance of community service
- To come up with some community service projects that you can participate in
- To complete the Healthy Masculinity Post-Test

Community Service Goals

Many people find it personally rewarding to become involved in their communities. A community is a unified body of people with common interests who live in a particular area. Implicit in this definition is a shared sense of responsibility for the welfare of the larger group. In other words, a community is no stronger than the level of commitment that its people have made to helping and protecting one another. Contributing to the welfare of others is part of the definition of being a "generative male."

Community Service Projects

Discuss with the group ways of becoming involved in the community. Brainstorm a list of potential community service projects that you can participate in. For example, perhaps you can participate in a local park clean-up effort. Or maybe there is a homeless shelter or food bank where you can donate your time. Work with your therapist to plan your community service.

Healthy Masculinity Post-Test

At the completion of the module, your therapist will once again administer a post-test to gauge your progress and determine whether you are ready to move on to the next phase of treatment. You therapist will hand out copies of the test in group.

Homework

- ✎ Use the worksheet provided to write a short essay about your community service goals.
- ✎ Be sure to bring your completed essay to the next meeting.
- ✎ Complete the Healthy Masculinity Post-Test prior to the next session.

My Community Service Goals

Goals

- To complete treatment and reflect on what you have learned
- To look toward the future

What's Next

In completing all of the modules in your treatment, you have worked hard and acquired important knowledge and life skills. To be successful in the future, you will need to consistently apply what you have learned. Remember, the more you put what you have learned into practice, the more that it will become a habit and seem natural to you. To help you remember what you have learned, and the importance of staying motivated, it is suggested that you complete the following worksheet. It is recommended that you keep the completed worksheet in a safe place, along with your relapse prevention plan. Both documents should be reviewed on a regular basis.

How I have changed as a person

Write a paragraph on changes that you have made since starting treatment. Do you like yourself better now than before? If the answer is "yes", explain why?

____

____

____

____

____

____

"What will likely happen to me if I fail?" Describe what is likely to happen if you were to sexually re-offend. What would be the potential consequences for you and the people who care most about you?

____

____

____

____

____

____

"What will likely happen to me if I succeed?" Describe what is likely to happen if you are successful in not re-offending and stick with your life plan? How would you feel about yourself, and how would the people who care most about you feel?

____

____

____

____

____

____

Explain why it is important to you to succeed. List four reasons.

1. ____
2. ____
3. ____
4. ____

CPSIA information can be obtained at www.ICGtesting.com
Printed in the USA
BVOW10s0942271015

424010BV00004B/7/P